D!RTY

GREEK

D!RTY®
GREEK

Everyday Slang from
"What's Up?" to "F*%# Off!"

CHRISTOS SAMARAS
illustrated by **LINDSAY MACK**

Ulysses Press

Published by:
Ulysses Press
P.O. Box 3440
Berkeley, CA 94703
www.ulyssespress.com

ISBN: 978-1-61243-025-6
Library of Congress Control Number: 2011934780

10 9 8 7 6 5 4 3 2

Acquisitions Editor: Keith Riegert
Managing Editor: Claire Chun
Project Editor: Alice Riegert
Greek Editor: Afroditi Ermidi
English proofreader: Lauren Harrison
Production: Jake Flaherty
Interior design: what!design @ whatweb.com
Cover design: Double R Design
Front cover photo: woman © konstantynov/shutterstock.com
Back cover illustration: Lindsay Mack

TABLE OF CONTENTS

USING THIS BOOK

Dirty Greek was written with the assumption that you already know at least enough Greek to get by. This is a slang book, after all, and you need to learn to walk before you can run. So if all the Greek you know came from above the front doors of the frat houses you used to stumble by on your way to your dorm, go get Rosetta Stone before you do anything stupid. Greek's been around for a very, very long time, so you need to spend at least a little time mastering the basics before you start cussing like a sailor. It's worth it though because you can really say some nasty shit in Greek.

So I'm going to assume that you can get yourself around the Greek language and you're ready to step your game up to a level usually reserved for downtown Athens after midnight. Having said that, it's very important to keep in mind that even though Greek can be very expressive and downright graphic, it's also old-fashioned in many ways. For example, do NOT go try out the new slang you learned in this book on someone older than you, especially if you don't know them. That is the quickest way to make yourself look like a total punk.

But after you leave grandma's house to go play count-the-empty-shot-glasses with your friends, then the slang will flow like wine or beer or ouzo. Start talking all proper here and everyone will look at you like you're a pompous douche. We don't want that at all, so I've made this book as user-friendly as possible, with the focus on proper pronunciation, as well as context. Words are given in English, Greeklish, and Greek, and each is also used in used in a sentence so you can understand when and how each word is used. The goal here is not just to teach you bad vocab, but to make you so comfortable with it that you'll be able to call the meter maid a fascist pig or tell that smokin' hot girl just how nice her legs are at the drop of a hat.

Okay, enough foreplay. Take your *Dirty Greek* and get dirty with it!

····Some Basics

Greek's been around for a couple thousand years, so there's been a lot of time for people to fuck with it. This means that Greek is not the easiest language to get the hang of. The vocabulary is huge and half the words are impossible to spell. It'll take some time to understand all the ins 'n' outs and ups 'n' downs, but here are a few basics that'll help you at least look the part a little quicker.

Εσύ vs Εσείς: Like French, Spanish, Russian, and many other languages, Greek has two pronouns for "you." There's the singular, informal **εσύ** (e-SEE) and the plural, formal

εσείς (e-SEES). This being a slang book, the plural **εσείς** really doesn't apply, but the informal/formal distinction is a very important one that needs to be made when speaking to people, especially strangers. If the person you're talking to is in an older age group, say closer to 40 than 30, always play it safe and take the formal route. Leave out the slang too. If the dude's cool, he'll let you know that you don't have to be formal with him.

Pronouncing Greek: This is a pet peeve of mine; it drives me up the wall and I'm using the soapbox I'm standing on to shout my complaints. In the English-speaking world, Greek is taught with what English scholars think is an ancient and therefore correct pronunciation of both letters and words. Never mind the fact that Greek scholars completely disagree with the proposed ancient pronunciation. But modern Greek is definitely not spoken this way. First of all, that "alpha beta gamma" shit sounds terrible by itself and a thousand times worse if you know how Greek should be pronounced. So, here's where we're going to learn how to sound like a local because, believe me, nothing will make you not get laid quicker than sounding like a dumb American or English tourist.

One important thing to remember is that Greek is spoken with an open mouth, meaning it's a little more full-bodied than English. There's no twang and it's less nasal than English. What this means for you is that when speaking, keep in mind that your mouth should stay more open and the tip of your tongue should be very close to the back of your teeth. It sounds weird, but it works. Take a look at the chart below and practice pronouncing the letters and their sounds for a little bit. Keep the mouth-tongue thing in mind, and your accent and pronunciation will instantly improve.

Αα	Alfa	Open up and say "aaahhh"
Ββ	Veeta	V as in Venus
Γγ	Wama	W as in "wonderful"
Δδ	Thelta	Th like "THe"
Εε	Epsilon	E as in "eskimo"
Ζζ	Zeeta	Z as in "zebra"
Ηη	Eeta	E as in "beep"
Θθ	Theeta	Th like "Thermos"
Ιι	Yiota	E as in "beep"
Κκ	Kappa	K as in "kite"

Λλ	Lamtha	L as in "love"
Μμ	Mee	M as in "moron"
Νν	Nee	N as in "night"
Ξξ	Xee	X as in "explode"
Οο	Omikron	O as in "oral"
Ππ	Pee	P as in "pencil"
Ρρ	Ro	Roll your R
Σσς	Sigma	S as in "sight"
Ττ	Taf	T as in "table"
Υυ	Eepsilon	E as in "beep"
Φφ	Fee	F as in "fish"
Χχ	Hee	H as in "whore"
Ψψ	Psi	Ps as in "psst"
Ωω	Omega	O as in "oral"

Diphtongs

Αι	E as in "eskimo"
Αυ	AF or AV as in "affect" or "available"
Ει	EE as in "beep"
Ευ	EF or EV as in "effort" or "forever"
Οι	EE as in "beep"
ου	OO as in "boob"

Double Consonants

| **γκ** | G as in "garage" |
| **γγ** | G as in "garage" |

μπ	B as in "bar"
ντ	D as in "dog"
τς	TS as in "cats"
τζ	J as in "jump"

Accents: I took four years of French in high school and to this day I have no idea how or when you use their accents. And since French relies heavily on its accents, this basically means that I just can't write in French, regardless of the fact that I speak enough to not be called a *stupeed Americen*. Thankfully Greek accents are easy to use. First of all there are only two: ´ and ¨. The accent is placed on the vowel that's stressed, so you basically always know how to pronounce the word. Single syllable words don't need accents since there's only one vowel to stress. The best thing, though, is that even if you miss an accent when you write, it's no big deal, because unlike French, Greek words don't have multiple meanings depending on where you place or don't place an accent. Take a look at the sentence below and you'll see how simple and informative Greek accents are.

I réally wish áccents were this éasy to understánd in óther lánguages.

See how easy? Where your voice perks up is where the accent goes. The other accent, ¨, serves to break up the diphthongs you saw before. For example, **αι** makes an "e" sound, but **αϊ** makes an "ay" sound as in **Αϊ-Βασίλης** (Santa Claus).

CHAPTER 1

HOWDY GREEK
EH-LEE-NEE-KEE HEH-REH-TEE-SMEE
Ελληνικοί Χαιρετισμοί

Before you can tell someone to fuck off, you need to be able to say hello to them first. Just like in most languages, saying hello (γεια σου; *YAH-soo*) is pretty straightforward and simple. The typical "hello" (γεια σου/σας; *YAH soo/sas*) and "how are you" (τι κάνεις/κάνετε; *tee KAH-nees/KAH-neh-teh*) applies the same way it does in English. The only thing that requires some brain power is to figure out whether you use the formal, plural (σας; *sas*) or informal, singular (σου; *soo*). As a general rule of thumb, if you are talking to someone you don't know that looks closer to 40 than 30, play it safe and stick with the formal, plural. They'll let you know real quick if being formal with them isn't necessary, but if you start off informal, you'll look like a punk with no social graces. With friends or young people, keep it informal or you'll sound like you have a stick up your ass.

You'll notice that the word ρε is used in many of the greetings below. ρε is something like an exclamation. You add it next to a word (e.g., *malaka*), to give it some emphasis. It's an easy way to give your speech a touch more slang and can be thrown into just about any sentence you can think of. Furthermore, some of the greetings below work better with ρε than without.

Hi!
YAH Soo!
Γεια σου!

Hi
Yi-A
Γεια

Hello
YIAH soo
Γεια σου

Ay
YIAH hah-ra-DAN
Γεια χαραντάν

Hey, dude.
***E-la**, re mal-A-ka.*
Έλα, ρε μαλάκα.

This phrase is said with minimal stress and very monotone. If you really spike the accents, the phrase becomes a little more confrontational, kinda like "Where the hell have you been?" or "It's about fucking time." You can also add the word μαλάκα (ma-LA-ka), if you want (see sidebar).

Sup.
Ehp.
Επ.

Howdy.
HEH-reh-teh.
Χαίρετε.
Can be as formal as "salutations," but more commonly used to be funny.

Welcome.
Ka-LOS tohn/Ka-LOS teen.
Καλώς τον/Καλώς την.

There he is./There she is.
NA-tohs./NA-tee.
Να 'τος./Να 'τη.
This is the informal version of "welcome," for when you don't feel like sounding like a pompous douche.

····What's up?
Tee YEE-neh-teh?
Τι γίνεται;

What's happening?
Tee Yee-neh-teh?
Τι γίνεται;

What would be happening?
Tee na YEE-nee?
Τι να γίνει;
This is a cool and popular way to say nothing or not much. Slightly mumble and you'll sound like a slick local every time.

What happened?
TEE EH-yee-neh (re)?
Τι έγινε (ρε);
If you want to ask someone "what the hell happened?" then you put some stress on it.

Hey man, what's the word?
EH-lah, re ma-LA-ka, tee LEH-ee?
Έλα, ρε μαλάκα, **τι λέει**;

What's new?
Tee NEH-ah?
Τι νέα;

What the dilly?
Tee ha-BA-ria?
Τι χαμπάρια;

> **What the dilly, guys?**
> *Ti ha-BA-ria, m-A-nges?*
> Τι χαμπάρια, μάγκες;
> If you want to emphasize someone's masculinity, ask 'em "what the dilly?"

····How are you?
POHS EE-seh?
Πώς είσαι;

What are you up to?
Tee KA-nees?
Τι κάνεις;
Most common way to say "how are you." The response will usually be "good" (*kah-LA*).

How's it going?
p-O-s p-A-ei?
Πώς πάει;

How are you doing?
POS ta p-A-s?
Πώς τα πας;

How you doin'?
POS pas?
Πώς πας;

All good?
OH-la ka-LAH?
Όλα καλά;

A very common phrase, usually combined with other greetings such as Έλα, ρε, όλα καλά; (*EH-la reh, OH-la ka-LAH?* / Hey dude, what's up, all good?) Or Τι γίνεται, όλα καλά; OH-la ka-LAH? (*ee YEE-neh-teh, OH-la ka-LAH?* / What's up, all good?)

Good.
Ka-LA.
Καλά.

All good.
OH-la Ka-LAH.
Όλα καλά.

Bitchin'.
KA-vla.
Καύλα.
Literally, "hard" or "hard-on." Use this when things are really good. You'll definitely be asked to elaborate.

It's all good.
OH-la j-E-t.
Όλα τζετ.
This is a really old school P.I.M.P. way to say it's all good.

So, so.
EH-tsee, KEH-tsee.
Έτσι κι έτσι.

Nothing.
TEE-poh-tah.
Τίποτα.

Bullshit.
Mah-la-KEEehs.
Μαλακίες.
Here is the ultimate Greek vocab word in one of its many, many uses. In this case, it is a typical response to Τι γίνεται (Tee GEE-neh-teh? / What's happening?), Τι νέα; (Tee NEH-ah? / What's new?), or Τι λέει; (Tee LEH-ee? / What's the word?). It's probably the most badass way to say nothing's going on. The English equivalent would be when you reply "shiiit" to something like "What's up?" or "What's new?"

How you doin', man?
Pohs EE-seh, reh FEE-leh?
Πώς είσαι, ρε φίλε;

> **The same.**
> *Ta EE-dee-ah.*
> Τα ίδια.

Same shit, different day.
Tah EE-thyah skah-TAH.
Τα ίδια σκατά.

Same old, same old.
Tah EE-thyah keh tah EE-thyah.
Τα ίδια και τα ίδια.

Shitty.
Skah-TA.
Σκατά.

Say it with some stress on the vowels, almost to the point where you break the word in two (*sk-Aaah-TAAH*).

Terrible.
HAHL-yah.
Χάλια.

If you want to get a shoulder to cry on, this would be how you would respond when someone asks you how you're doing. Say this with as sad a face as possible and you'll immediately get asked to elaborate.

I'm in trouble.
EH-hoh BLEH-ksee.
Έχω μπλέξει.

This is reserved for when you want to tell a friend that you've gotten into some shit that you don't want to be in, and really need some help to get out of.

····In the a.m.
Toh Poohr-NOH
Το πουρνό

Good morning.
Kah-leeMEH-rah.
Καλημέρα.

Mornin'!
MEH-rah!
Μέρα!

You need to stop jacking off in the morning!

PREH-pee nah KOH-psees teen proh-ee-NEE mah-la-KEE-ah!

Πρέπει να κόψεις την πρωινή μαλακία!

This is a great phrase to use with a friend that's still groggy and not really responding to the conversation.

Looks like someone got up on the wrong side of the bed!

LEE-ghoh ah-yhoo-roh-ksee-pnee-MEH-nohs EE EH-tsee moo FEH-neh-the?

Λίγο αγουροξυπνημένος ή έτσι μου φαίνεται;

I feel awful this morning.

Ehs-THAH-no-meh HAHL-yah SEE-meh-rah.

Αισθάνομαι χάλια σήμερα.

••••In the p.m.

Toh VRAH-thee

Το Βράδυ

Good evening.
Kah-lee-SPEH-rah.
Καλησπέρα.

Good night!
Kah-leeNEE-htah!
Καληνύχτα!

Have a nice night.
Kah-LOH VRAH-thee.
Καλό βράδυ.

Sweet dreams.
OH-nee-rah yhlee-KA.
Όνειρα γλυκά.

····Please
Se pah-rah-kal-O
Σε παρακαλώ

Come on man.
E-la re FEE-le.
Έλα, ρε φίλε.

This exact same phrase is a simple greeting but it is also used to say "please." Put more stress on the first vowel when you say this phrase.

Hook a brother up.
KAH-neh moo tee HAH-ree.
Κάνε μου τη χάρη.

This phrase is used when you're exasperated and trying to get someone to cooperate with you.

Hook me up.
Ka-NOH-nee-seh.
Κανόνισε.

Can you do me a favor?
Moo KAH-nees MEE-ah HAH-ree?
Μου κάνεις μία χάρη;

····Thank you
Eh-fhah-ree-STOH
Ευχαριστώ

Thanks!
Seh-fhah-ree-STOH!
Σ' ευχαριστώ!

May you be well, dude.
NA-se kal-A, *re.*
Να 'σαι καλά, ρε.

This is a common way of saying "thanks," especially if you want to show a little bit more gratitude than usual. You can also use this phrase to say "you're welcome."

Right on dude, thanks for the help.
So-STOS, reh, **seh-fha-ree-STO yia tee vo-EE-thee-ah.**
Σωστός, ρε, **σ' ευχαριστώ για τη βοήθεια**.

You're welcome.
Pah-rah-kah-LOH
Παρακαλώ.

This is the official way to say "you're welcome" and it's commonplace among strangers, but rarely used between friends.

You're the man.
EE-seh PROH-tohs.
Είσαι πρώτος.

No problem.
Kah-NEH-nah PROHV-lee-mah.
Κανένα πρόβλημα.

You could also say "no problem" in a Greek accent, or you could just say "nothing," (*TEE-poh-tah*/τίποτα).

I got you, bro.
SEH-hoh, reh ah-THER-feh.
Σ' έχω, ρε αδερφέ.

····Sorry/My apologies
See-NGHNOH-mee
Συγνώμη

The Greek word for "sorry" is συγνώμη (see-NGHNOH-mee). You'd think that this word would be reserved for when you're really fucking sorry, but even then the English "sorry" is OK. Just say it like you mean it.

Sorry.
SOH-ree.
Σόρι.

My mistake.
LAH-thohs moo.
Λάθος μου.

Usually combined with "sorry," for example, σόρι λάθος (*SOH-ree LAH-thohs*).

It's my fault.
Eg-O FTEH-oH.
Εγώ φταίω.

My bad.
Ma-la-KEE-ah moo.
Μαλακία μου.

Excuse me.
Meh Seen-hoh-REE-teh.
Με συγχωρείτε.

····I don't care
Then mehn-thyah-FEH-ree
Δεν μ' ενδιαφέρει

I don't give a shit.
HEH-stee-ka.
Χέστηκα.

Literally, "I shat myself." You're
basically sarcastically saying
that what you just heard was so
intense, important, or interesting
that you took a dump in your
pants.

I don't give a fuck.
Stohn POO-tsoh moo.
Στον πούτσο μου.

Literally, "to my dick." You can
symbolically direct a lot of things
you don't care about toward your
junk.

Fuck if I care.
Stahr-HEE-thya moo.
Στ' αρχίδια μου.

Literally, "my nuts." The most common way to say "I don't care."

I don't give a flying fuck.
Stah pah-PAHR-yia moo.
Στα παπάρια μου.

I don't give a dime.
Then THEE-noh theh-KAH-rah.
Δεν δίνω δεκάρα.

I don't give a dick.
Then THEE-noh EH-nan POO-tsoh.
Δεν δίνω έναν πούτσο.

I don't give a rat's ass!
NAH!
Να!

This phrase is almost always accompanied by bringing your
hand down right next to your crotch in a slow mo karate chop.

....I don't know
Then KSEH-roh
Δεν ξέρω

I don't understand.
Then kah-tah-lah-VEH-noh.
Δεν καταλαβαίνω.

I don't get you.
Then seh kah-tah-lah-VEH-noh.
Δεν σε καταλαβαίνω.

I don't know what the fuck is going on.
EH-hoh HAH-see teen BAH-lah.
Έχω χάσει την μπάλα.

I don't have a clue.
Then EH-hoh ee-THEH-ah.
Δεν έχω ιδέα.

What'd I miss?
Tee EH-hah-sah?
Τι έχασα;

What don't I know?
Tee then KSEH-roh?
Τι δεν ξέρω;

....Nice to meet you
HAH-ree-kah
Χάρηκα

Most Greeks tend to be very open and friendly when you first meet them. It might get a little intense if you're a white guy from the burbs, but it really does give you a nice, warm feeling once you get over the potential initial awkwardness.

Have you two met?
EH-heh-teh ksa-nah-ghnoh-ree-STEE eh-SEES ee THEE-oh?

Έχετε ξαναγνωριστεί εσείς οι δύο;

Do you know...?
KSEH-rees tohn/teen...?
Ξέρεις τον/την...;
All you have to do is pick a gender and add a name.

What's your name?
Pohs seh LEH-neh?
Πώς σε λένε;

> #### My name is Dimitri and I'm here to party!
> *Meh LEH-neh Thee-MEE-tree keh EE-rthah nah tah SPA-soh!*
> Με λένε Δημήτρη και ήρθα να τα σπάσω!

What was your name again?
Pohs EE-pah-meh toh OH-noh-MA-soo?
Πώς είπαμε το όνομά σου;

Nice talking to you.
HAH-ree-ka poo tah EE-pah-meh.
Χάρηκα που τα είπαμε.

Let's go...
PAh-meh ...
Πάμε...

> #### get some coffee.
> *yah kah-FEH.*
> για καφέ.
>
> #### out.
> *EH-lah nah VGHOO-meh.*
> έλα να βγούμε.
>
> #### chill.
> *nah-RA-ksoo-meh.*
> ν' αράξουμε.
>
> #### outside.
> *EH-ksoh.*
> έξω.
>
> #### for a walk/ride/drive.
> *VOHL-tah.*
> βόλτα.

lay down.

nah ksa-PLOH-soo-meh.

να ξαπλώσουμε.

This one's usually used between people who are sleeping together because it's slightly sexual. You can say it to the girl you're trying to get in bed, but I can't promise you anything.

····Bye!

Yah!

Γεια!

Good-bye.

YAH soo.

Γεια σου.

See ya!

Tah LEH-meh!

Τα λέμε!

I'm out.

Teen EK-ha-na.

Την έκανα.

I gotta run.

PREH-pee nah teen KAH-noh.

Πρέπει να την κάνω.

Time to go…

OH-rah nah FEE-ghoo-meh…

Ώρα να φύγουμε…

I'm outta here.

Teen KAH-noh.

Την κάνω.

See you soon.

Tah LEH-meh SEE-doh-mah.

Τα λέμε σύντομα.

Deuces.

TSAH-yiah.

Τσάγια.

CHAPTER 2

FRIENDLY GREEK
FEE-LEE-KAH E-LEE-NEE-KAH
Φιλικά ελληνικά

Greeks are open and talkative people. Some are friendlier than others, but just about everyone you run into will be more than happy to shoot the shit with you. If you return the favor, and are good with the words, you'll definitely earn yourself a big group of friends to hang out with. Don't get it twisted though: many people will be extremely friendly and open with you, but that doesn't necessarily mean they got your back. Just like every other place on the planet, this kind of friendship takes some time.

There are different words, phrases, and terms of endearment that you use depending on what kind of relationship you have with each person, but don't forget that μαλάκα (*ma-LA-ka*; dude) can be used for pretty much anyone at any time.

····Friends

FEE-lee
Φίλοι

Dimitra is my friend from high school.
*EE THEE-mee-trah EE-neh **FEE-lee** moo AP-to LEE-kee-oh.*
Η Δήμητρα είναι **φίλη** μου απ' το λύκειο.

George is my friend. He'll definitely let us go backstage.
*Oh YIOH-rghos EE-neh **FEE-lohs** moo. SEE-ghoo-ra thah mas ah-FEE-see na PA-meh sta pah-rah-SKEE-nya.*
Ο Γιώργος είναι **φίλος** μου. Σίγουρα θα μας αφήσει να πάμε στα παρασκήνια.

I haven't seen my friends in a month.
*Then EH-ho thee toos **FEE-loos** moo yiah EH-na MEE-na.*
Δεν έχω δει τους **φίλους** μου για ένα μήνα.

Mike is my best friend!
*Oh mee-HAH-lees EE-neh oh **ka-LEE-teh-ros moo FEE-los**!*
Ο Μιχάλης είναι ο **καλύτερος μου φίλος**!

I think you and I are going to be good friends.
*Noh-MEE-zoh pohs eh-GHOH keh see thah GEE-noo-meh **kah-LEE FEE-lee**.*
Νομίζω πως εγώ κι εσύ θα γίνουμε **καλοί φίλοι**.

Those two are inseparable.
Af-TEE ee THEE-oh EE-neh KOH-lohs keh vrah-KEE.
Αυτοί οι δύο είναι κώλος και βρακί.
Κώλος means "ass" and βρακί is "underwear"…get it?

Bro, have I got a story to tell you…
***Ah-ther-FEH**, EH-hoh MEE-ah ee-stohr-EE-ah nah soo poh…*
Αδερφέ, έχω μία ιστορία να σου πω...

My roommate is so messy.
Oh see-GAH-tee-kohs moo EE-neh vroh-MYAH-rees.
Ο **συγκάτοικός** μου είναι βρομιάρης.

I really don't like my classmates.
Then moo a-REH-soon ka-THO-loo ee see-mah-thee-TES moo.
Δεν μου αρέσουν καθόλου οι **συμμαθητές** μου.

I'm going out with the group.
Tha vgo me teen pa-REH-ah mou.
Θα βγω με την **παρέα** μου.

We got into a fight because I wanted to go out with the guys.
Tsa-ko-THEE-ka-meh eh-pee-THEE EE-theh-la na vgoh me ta peh-THIA.
Τσακωθήκαμε επειδή ήθελα να βγω με τα **παιδιά**.

My girlfriend is pissed off at me but I don't know why.
Ee koh-PEH-la moo EE-neh tsa-dees-MEH-nee ma-ZEE moo, ah-LA then KSEH-roh yah-TEE.
Η **κοπέλα** μου είναι τσαντισμένη μαζί μου, αλλά δεν ξέρω γιατί.

My crazy boyfriend just bought a fucking motorcycle!
Toh moor-LOH ah-GHOH-ree moo MOH-lees PEE-reh MEE-a gah-moh-mee-hah-NEE!
Το μουρλό **αγόρι** μου μόλις πήρε μία γαμω-μηχανή!

WANKER)))
MA-LA-KAS
ΜΑΛΑΚΑΣ

If you remember nothing else from this book, remember the word *malaka(s)*. Successfully master how to use this gem of the Greek language and there's half your bag of slang right there. If you don't get a handle on using it, you might as well stay on the plane.

The literal definition of *malakas* is. . .wait for it—a chronic masturbator. You know, someone who whacks it way too much and way too hard. Of course, the word is rarely ever used for its literal translation; in ancient times meant "sick." Today, it has a laundry list of uses, ranging from the all-time classic "stupid," to "dude." Throw it in as often as possible to add some flava to the conversation.

What's up dude, how did you get home from the bar last night?
Tee YEE-neh-teh, re ma-LA-ka, pos YEE-ree-ses ap-TOH bar?
Τι γίνεται, ρε **μαλάκα**, πώς γύρισες σπίτι απ' το μπαρ χθες το βράδυ;

Come on girl, let's go to the mall. I'm too bored to go by myself.
EH-la, mo-REE ma-LA-ko, PA-meh sto mol. Var-YEH-meh na PA-o MO-nee moo.
Έλα, μωρή **μαλάκω**, πάμε στο μολ. Βαριέμαι να πάω μόνη μου.

I told the idiot that there was no way I would go to my ex's house party.
Tou EE-pa tou ma-LA-ka otee then EH-peh-zeh na PA-o stees PROH-een moo to PAR-tee.
Του είπα του **μαλάκα** ότι δεν έπαιζε να πάω στης πρώην μου το πάρτι.

Stay for one drink dude, don't be a party pooper.
KA-tseh yia E-na poh-TOH, reh, meen EE-seh ma-LA-kas.
Κάτσε για ένα ποτό, ρε, μην είσαι **μαλάκας**.

You are a total **asshole**.
*EE-seh po-LA kee-LA **ma-LA-kas***.
Είσαι πολλά κιλά **μαλάκας**.

She didn't give it up last night so I had to **whack it** before I
went to sleep.
*Then MOO-ka-tse ee GOH-meh-nah hthes to VRA-thee keh
EH-preh-peh **na tra-VEE-kso MEE-ah ma-la-KI-ah** preen
kee-mee-THO.*
Δεν μου 'κατσε η γκόμενα χθες το βράδυ και έπρεπε
να τραβήξω μια μαλακία πριν κοιμηθώ.

The pizza **sucked**. I didn't like it at all.
***Ma-la-KI-ah** ee PEE-tsa. Then moo A-reh-seh ka-THO-loo.*
Μαλακία η πίτσα. Δεν μου άρεσε καθόλου.

This is **bullshit**. There's no way I'm going to pay this ticket.
*Tee **ma-la-KI-es** EE-neh af-TES? A-poh-KLEE-eh-teh na
plee-ROH-soh af-TEE teen KLEE-see.*
Τι **μαλακίες** είναι αυτές; Αποκλείεται να πληρώσω
αυτή την κλήση.

The **stupid bitch** couldn't even turn on the laptop.
*Then boh-ROO-seh na-NEE-ksee to LAP-top ee **ma-la-keez-
MEH-nee**.*
Δεν μπορούσε ν' ανοίξει το λάπτοπ η **μαλακισμένη**.

I just bought the **piece of shit** and it doesn't even work!
*MO-lees to PEE-ra to **ma-la-keez-MEH-no** ke then thoo-
LEH-vee!*
Μόλις το πήρα το **μαλακισμένο** και δεν δουλεύει!

I'm **fucking up dude**. I have a great girl and I'm still talking
to other ones.
***Ma-la-KEEZ-oo-meh**, re **ma-LA-ka**. E-ho ka-LEE ko-PEH-la
ke teen PEF-to se A-les.*
Μαλακίζομαι, ρε **μαλάκα**. Έχω καλή κοπέλα και την
πέφτω σε άλλες.

····Family

ee-ko-YEH-nee-ah
Οικογένεια

My parents told me to get my lazy ass out of the house and find my own apartment.
Ee goh-NEES moo moo EE-pan na kse-koo-bees-STOH AP-toh SPEE-tee ke na vro dee-KO moo dia-MER-eez-ma.
Οι **γονείς** μου μου είπαν να ξεκουμπιστώ απ' το σπίτι και να βρω δικό μου διαμέρισμα.

Jesus Christ, Mom, you don't know how to knock?
Kah-LAH, reh MAH-nah, then KSEH-rees nah htee-PAS?
Καλά, ρε **μάνα**, δεν ξέρεις να χτυπάς;

My dad doesn't like my girlfriend.
Oh pa-TEH-ras moo then PA-ee teen GO-meh-na moo.
Ο **πατέρας** μου δεν πάει την γκόμενά μου.

I want my **mommy/daddy**!!!
THE-lo tee ma-MA/ton ba-BA moo!!!
Θέλω **τη μαμά**/τον **μπαμπά** μου!!!

My old man is hounding me to get a job.
Oh YEH-ros moo moo ta PREE-zee na vro thoo-LIA.
Ο **γέρος** μου μου τα πρήζει να βρω δουλειά.

Grandpa and **Grandma** gave me 100 Euros for Christmas.
Oh pa-POOS ke ee yia-YIA moo E-thoh-san eh-kah-TO eh-VROH yia ta hree-STOO-yeh-nah.
Ο **παππούς** και η **γιαγιά** μου έδωσαν €100 ευρώ για τα Χριστούγεννα.

My aunt and **uncle** are getting a divorce.
Ho-REE-zoon ee THEE-ah ke oh THEE-os mou.
Χωρίζουν η **θεία** και ο **θείος** μου.

My own **sister** just cock blocked me.
Ee EE-dia moo ee ah-ther-FEE moo EH-kah-neh hah-LA-strah.
Η ίδια μου η **αδερφή** μού έκανε χαλάστρα.

Dude, I passed out on the couch and my **brother** shaved my eyebrow.
*Ma-LA-ka, me PEE-reh oh EE-pnos ston kah-nah-PEH keh oh **ah-ther-FOS** moo moo KSEE-ree-seh to FREE-dee.*
Μαλάκα, με πήρε ο ύπνος στον καναπέ και ο **αδερφός** μου μου ξύρισε το φρύδι.

Come on, **bro**, I'm dying! Please hook me up with your **cousin**.
*EH-la, re **ah-Ther-FE**, then an-DEH-ho AH-lo. Pleez, FTIAH-kseh meh meh teen **ksah-THER-fee** soo.*
Έλα, ρε **αδερφέ**, δεν αντέχω άλλο. Πλιζ, φτιάξε με με την **ξαδέρφη** σου.

····At work, and out and about
Stee thoo-LIA ke EH-kso, tree-YEE-roh
Στη δουλειά και έξω, τριγύρω

My **boss** is the biggest asshole I've ever met.
*Toh **ah-fen-dee-KOH** moo EE-neh oh pee-OH meh-GAH-los ma-LA-kas poo EH-hoh thee stee zoh-EE moo.*
Το **αφεντικό** μου είναι ο πιο μεγάλος μαλάκας που έχω δει στη ζωή μου.

I like my **coworkers**. They're a good group of
people.
*EE-neh en-DAH-ksee AH-toh-mah ee **seen-AH-thel-fee**
moo. Toos PAH-o.*
Είναι εντάξει άτομα οι **συνάδελφοί** μου. Τους πάω.

Do you know that **guy**?
*Tohn KSEH-rees ahf-TOH tohn **tee-PA**?*
Τον ξέρεις αυτό τον **τυπά**;

Dude check out that **babe** across the street.
*Ma-LA-ka, KEE-tah toh **pee-PEE-nee** ah-PEH-nah-dee.*
Μαλάκα, κοίτα το **πιπίνι** απέναντι.

Can you call the **waiter/waitress** for me?
*Bo-REES na foh-NA-ksees ton **ser-vee-TOH-roh**/tee
ser-vee-TOH-ra?*
Μπορείς να φωνάξεις τον **σερβιτόρο**/τη **σερβιτόρα**;

I think that **cop** is about to pull you over.
*Noh-MEE-zoh pos af-TOHS oh **BAH-tsohs** tha seh stah-
ma-TEE-see.*
Νομίζω πως αυτός ο **μπάτσος** θα σε σταματήσει.

The **bartender** at Destille makes the best drinks.
*Oh **BAHR-mahn** stoh Destille KAH-nee ta kah-LEE-teh-
rah poh-TA.*
Ο **μπάρμαν** στο Destille κάνει τα καλύτερα ποτά.
Say μπαρούμαν (bahr-WOO-mahn) if your mixologist is
of female persuasion.

My brother's the **bouncer**. He'll let us in for sure.
*Oh ah-ther-FOS mou kanei **POR-ta**. SEE-yoo-RA thah
mas VAH-lee MEH-sa.*
Ο αδερφός μου κάνει **πόρτα**. Σίγουρα θα μας βάλει
μέσα.

Dude, I think the **stripper** stole my wallet.
*Reh ma-LA-ka, no-MEE-zo oh-TEE ee **streep-tee-ZOO**
MOO-fa-geh to por-to-FO-lee.*
Ρε μαλάκα, νομίζω πως η **στριπτιζού** μού 'φαγε το
πορτοφόλι.

····More than friends
KAH-tee pa-ra-PA-no AH-po FEE-lee
Κάτι παραπάνω από φίλοι

All of Greece's sand and sun makes for a very horny environment. Hell, even the ancient ruins and stray dogs add to the country's sexiness, so go ahead and try your luck with the locals. Hooking up in Greece is like landing a plane—it's all about the approach. Guys, humor and confidence are your best weapons, but don't forget to pay for absolutely everything, no matter how much the girl protests. And ladies, don't be standoffish, or you'll run the risk of being perceived as a total bitch. The guys do all the work but you've gotta give them some sort of a green light, ladies.

My god, he's gorgeous.
*Theh moo, EE-neh **KOO-klohs**.*
Θεέ μου, είναι **κούκλος**.

I'm over pretty boys. The next one's going to be a brute.
*Vah-REH-thee-ka tah **oh-mor-FOH-peh-tha**. Oh eh-POH-meh-nohs thah EE-neh **AH-drah-klahs**.*
Βαρέθηκα τα **ομορφόπαιδα**. Ο επόμενος θα είναι **άντρακλας**.

Listen, I'm not very handsome, but I'm a nice guy.
*AH-koo, then EE-meh poh-LEE OH-mor-fohs, ah-LAH EE-meh **kah-LOH peh-THEE**.*
Άκου, δεν είμαι πολύ όμορφος, αλλά είμαι **καλό παιδί**.

I finally got myself a strapping young man.
*Eh-pee-THE-loos, VREE-kah keh-YHO EH-nan **peh-thah-RA**.*
Επιτέλους, βρήκα κι εγώ έναν **παιδαρά**.

I don't mean to be a dick, but she's way too pretty for you.

*Then THEH-loh na fah-NOH ma-LA-kas, ah-LA EE-neh poh-LEE **OH-mohr-fee** yia SEH-na.*

Δεν θέλω να φανώ μαλάκας, αλλά είνα πολύ **όμορφη** για σένα.

Jesus Christ that girl is so hot.

*Pa-na-YEE-ah moo, tee **moo-NA-ra** EE-tahn af-TEE!*

Παναγία μου, τι **μουνάρα** ήταν αυτή!

Παναγία is actually Virgin Mary, not J.C.

Baby, you are beautiful.

*Moh-ROH moo, EE-she **pah-NEH-mohr-fee**.*

Μωρό μου, είσαι **πανέμορφη**.

This chick is costing me a lot of money.

*MOO kohs-TEE-zee poh-LAH lef-TA af-TEE ee **GOH-meh-na**.*

Μου κοστίζει πολλά λεφτά αυτή η **γκόμενα**.

You'll hear γκόμενα thrown around all over the place. I like it because of how it came about. Back in the day when Greek merchant or naval ships would dock at some port, the sailors would go looking for whores and use their terrible English. More specifically, they would ask where they could find the women that "go with men." "Go" and "men" eventually got stuck together to make GO-MEN-ah, or γκόμενα. Cool, huh?

Kylie looks unbelievable in that dress.

*Ee KAHEE-lee EE-neh **ah-PEE-steff-tee** mahf-TOH toh FOH-reh-ma.*

Η Κάιλι είναι **απίστευτη** μ' αυτό το φόρεμα.

"Unbelievable" is the literal translation, but use this if you're trying to say something like "stunning," "ridiculous," or "super hot."

I just can't get over how sexy you look when you dance like that.

*Then boh-ROH na xeh-peh-RAH-soh toh POH-soh **SEH-xee** EE-she OH-tahn hoh-REH-vees EH-tsee.*

Δεν μπορώ να ξεπεράσω το πόσο **σέξι** είσαι όταν χορεύεις έτσι.

I think **we're dating**, but I'm not a hundred percent sure.
*Noh-MEE-zoh pohs **TAH'-hoo-meh**, ah-LAH then EE-meh eh-kah-TOH tees eh-kah-TOH SEE-yhoo-rohs.*
Νομίζω πως **τα 'χουμε**, αλλά δεν είμαι εκατό τοις εκατό σίγουρος.

We just **broke up**. Single at last!
*MOH-lees **hoh-REE-sa-meh**. Eh-pee-TEH-loos MOH-nohs!*
Μόλις **χωρίσαμε**. Επιτέλους μόνος!

I hit on the ethics teacher.
***Teen EH-peh-sa** steen kah-thee-YEE-tree-ah three-ske-ftee-KON.*
Την έπεσα στην καθηγήτρια θρησκευτικών.

I hooked up with my **ex** last night.
*Fah-SOH-thee-ka meh tohn **PROH-een** moo hthes to VRA-thee.*
Φασώθηκα με τον **πρώην** μου χθες το βράδυ.

I'm in a **slump**, bring me anything
*EH-hoh **ah-yha-MEE-es**, FEH-reh moo oh-tee NA-neh.*
Εχω **αγαμίες**, φέρε μου ό,τι να 'ναι.

I forgot we had a **date** tonight.
*KSEH-ha-sa pohs EE-hah-meh **rahn-deh-VOO** ah-PO-pseh.*
Ξέχασα πως είχαμε **ραντεβού** απόψε.

No, dude, it was just a **booty call**.
*OH-hee, reh, ah-PLOH **wan NA-eet stahnd** EE-than.*
Όχι, ρε, απλό **ουάν νάιτ σταντ** ήταν.

Can't I just have a **fuck buddy**?
*Then boh-ROH na EH-hoh ah-PLOHS EH-na **fak BA-dee**?*
Δεν μπορώ να έχω απλώς ένα **φακ μπάντι**;

Who says "**lover**" anymore?
*Pyohs LEH-ee "**eh-rah-STEE**" pyah?*
Ποιος λέει «**εραστή**» πια;

What's your sign?
*TEE **ZOH-thee**-oh EE-seh?*
Τι **ζώδιο** είσαι;

····That's kewwwwl
Ga-MAAAAA-ee
Γαμάαααααααει

There are quite a few ways to say something is cool in Greek. All are pretty much interchangeable and people tend to favor one or two words more than others. The choice is really up to you and what you like.

Sometimes I don't know what I like and what I don't like.
*Meh-ree-KES foh-RES then KSEH-roh tee **moo ah-REH-see** keh tee **then moo ah-REH-see**.*
Μερικές φορές δεν ξέρω τι **μου αρέσει** και τι **δεν μου αρέσει**.

I really dig Bob Marley's shit dude.
***Ghoo-STA-roh** poh-LEE tohn Bohb MAHR-lee reh FEE-le.*
Γουστάρω πολύ τον Μπομπ Μάρλεϊ, ρε φίλε.
Definitely the most popular way of saying like, other than "I like."

I'm dying for a cigarette.
***peh-THEH-noh** yia tsee-GHAH-roh.*
Πεθαίνω για τσιγάρο.
Quiting sucks balls, dude.

I kinda get off on seeing crashes, injuries...you know, that kind of stuff.
*Psee-LOH **FTYA-hno-meh** oh-TAHN VLEH-poh ah-tee-HEE-ma-ta, trahv-ma-TEE-es...KSEH-rees, THE-tya PRAGH-ma-ta.*
Ψιλο-**φτιάχνομαι** όταν βλέπω ατυχήματα, τραυματίες... ξέρεις, τέτοια πράγματα.

ONLY iN GREECE)))
MO-NOH STEEN EH-LA-THA
ΜΟΝΟ ΣΤΗΝ ΕΛΛΑΔΑ

Super Greek
Eh-lee-NA-ras

Ελληνάρας

A "super Greek" is someone who's too patriotic and too stuck in traditional and more old-fashioned ways. This can include taste in music, style, recreational activities, and interaction with one's family.

> That **super Greek** thought it was okay to watch the game while we were fucking.
> *Af-TOS oh **eh-lee-NA-ras** no-mee-zeh pos bo-ROO-seh na VLE-pee BA-la eh-NO pee-THYO-mas-tan.*
> Αυτός ο **Ελληνάρας** νόμιζε πως μπορούσε να βλέπει μπάλα ενώ πηδιόμασταν.

To fuck ass
Yha-MA-ee

Γαμάει

Sometimes, something (or someone) is so good, so cool, so amazing, so out of this world thatƐit fucks asses.

> My new laptop **fucks asses**.
> *Toh ke-NOOR-yoh moo LAHP-tohp **yha-MA-ee**.*
> Το καινούργιο μου λάπτοπ **γαμάει**.

The world is burning and the pussy is combing itself.
Oh KOZ-mos ke-yeh-teh ke toh moo-NEE hte-nee-zeh-teh.

Ο κόσμος καίγεται και το μουνί χτενίζεται.

This is the absolute best way to tell someone they are being dramatic about unimportant shit in ANY language.

Made a hell of a mess.
Tees poo-TAH-nas toh KA-geh-loh.

Της πουτάνας το κάγκελο.

When a situation gets out of hand, either in a good or bad way, it's common to describe the mess as "the whore's fence post." Back in the day at the docks, each whore had her fence post near the ships. If anyone else tried to mess with her turf, there would be hell to pay.

Fag
POO-stees
Πούστης
In this case, "fag" is used as a compliment. When someone does something impressive, unique, or just very well, they're called a "fag." Not literally, of course. The connection is made for the uniqueness and not the sexuality of a fag...I think.

Did you see how that **fag** just fooled the entire defense?
*EE-thes pohs kseh-YEH-la-seh OH-lee teen AH-mee-na oh **POO-stees**?*
Είδες πώς ξεγέλασε όλη την άμυνα ο **πούστης**;

Gay shit
Poo-STYAH
Πουστιά
If someone does something sneaky or dishonest for their own gain, they're said to have committed a gay act.

He did some **gay shit** with his paperwork and ended up not paying any taxes.
*EH-ka-neh **poo-STYAH** meh tah hahr-TYA too keh then PLEE-roh-seh TEE-poh-ta seh FOH-roos.*
Έκανε **πουστιά** με τα χαρτιά του και δεν πλήρωσε τίποτα σε φόρους.

Just go buy her a similar-looking cat and you'll be cool.
*PEE-yeh-neh PAHR-tees MEE-ah pahr-OH-mya GHA-ta keh THAH-seh **dzeht**.*
Πήγαινε πάρ' της μία παρόμοια γάτα και θα 'σαι **τζετ**.

Your car is so awesome, I'm kind of jealous.
***Gha-MAH-ee** toh ah-MA-xee soo, psee-loh-zee-LE-voh.*
Γαμάει το αμάξι σου, ψιλοζηλεύω.

This sound system kills!
***Ta SPAH-ee** toh ee-ho-SEE-stee-ma!*
Τα σπάει το ηχοσύστημα!

Have you seen Olympiakos's new center forward? The kid's fucking awesome.

*EH-hees thee tohn keh-NOOR-yoh SED-er fohr too oh-leem-pee-ah-KOO? **Gah-MAH-ee KOH-loos** toh peh-THEE.*

Έχεις δει τον καινούργιο σεντερ φορ του Ολυμπιακού; **Γαμάει κώλους** το παιδί.

Olympiakos (Ολυμπιακός) is the most successful soccer team in Greek history, and one of the most popular teams in the country. Their main rival is Panathinaikos (Παναθηναϊκός). More on that in Sporty Greek.

This gyro is so good it's making me hard.

***SKEH-tee KAHV-la** toh soo-VLA-kee.*

Σκέτη καύλα το σουβλάκι.

I'm not cool with garlic.

***Meh ha-LA-ee** toh SKOR-thoh.*

Με χαλάει το σκόρδο.

Dude, that guy just doesn't give a fuck.

Ma-LA-ka, af-TOS then EH-hee ton theh-OH too.

Μαλάκα, αυτός **δεν έχει τον θεό του**.

When someone just doesn't give a shit and is acting a fool, it is said that "he doesn't have his God."

I got so angry that I became furious.

*Tsa-DEE-stee-ka po-LEE **EH-yee-na TOOR-kos**.*

Τσαντίστηκα πολύ **έγινα Τούρκος**.

When someone gets really angry and they're screaming and foaming at the mouth, in Greece it's known as becoming a Turk. Yup, not big fans of the Turks.

It's Friday night and nowhere to go. We're fucking pathetic!

*Pah-rah-skeh-VEE VRAH-thee keh then EH-hoo-meh poo nah-PAH-meh. EE-ma-steh **yia tohn POO-tsoh**!*

Παρασκευή βράδυ και δεν έχουμε πού να πάμε. Είμαστε **για τον πούτσο**!

What kind of bullshit is this!?

*Tee **ma-la-KEE-es** EE-neh af-TES!?*

Τι **μαλακίες** είναι αυτές;

You'll hear this phrase a lot.

Dude, I was scared shitless!
Ma-LA-ka, HES-tee-ka PA-noh moo!
Μαλάκα, **χέστηκα πάνω μου**!

José Cuervo absolutely wrecks me.
Meh ghah-MAHee te-LEE-os toh Hoh-ZEH koo-ERV-oh.
Με **γαμάει** τελείως το Χοσέ Κουέρβο.

All tequila is harsh, but José especially is an evil bitch. Be prepared for it though since most places only have Cuervo, or even worse, El Jimador.

Don't piss me off.
Mee moo SPAS tah-RHEE-thia.
Μη **μου σπας τ' αρχίδια**.

It got so bad, you should've been there.
EH-yee-neh toh EH-la na thees.
Έγινε το έλα να δεις.

••••Characters
Tee-PAH-thes
Τυπάδες

There's definitely a lot of these in Greece, and there are just as many interesting ways to describe them.

THE GOOD...

He is a god on the guitar.
EE-neh theh-OHS steen kee-THAH-rah.
Είναι **θεός** στην κιθάρα.

My little brother is a really good kid.
Oh mee-kros moo ah-ther-FOS EE-neh po-LEE ka-LO peh-THEE.
Ο μικρός μου αδερφός είναι πολύ **καλό παιδί**.

Wow, look at that strapping young man.
Ah-MAN, KEE-tah af-TOH toh pa-lee-KA-ree.
Αμάν, κοίτα αυτό το **παλικάρι**.

Come on, run that red if you're such a badass.
EH-la, reh, PEH-ra-seh to KO-kee-no, AH-ma EE-seh MA-gas.
Έλα, ρε, πέρασε το κόκκινο, άμα είσαι **μάγκας**.

My girlfriend's dad is a real OG.
Oh pa-TEH-ras tees koh-PEH-lahs moo EE-neh po-LEE Vah-REES keh Ah-SEE-ko-tos.
Ο πατέρας της κοπέλας μου είναι πολύ **βαρύς και ασήκωτος**.

That rocker smells like bud and booze.
AF-tos oh roh-KAS vro-MA-ee FOO-da ke KSEE-thia.
Αυτός ο **ροκάς** βρομάει φούντα και ξίδια.

Thanks for the help, you're the best.
Seh-fha-ree-STOH yia tee voh-EE-thee-ah, EE-seh PROH-tohs.
Σ' ευχαριστώ για τη βοήθεια, είσαι **πρώτος**.

I can't believe you did that! You're one in a million.
Then pee-STEH-vo tee EH-ka-nes! EE-seh ah-ne-pa-NA-leep-tos.
Δεν πιστεύω τι έκανες! Είσαι **ανεπανάληπτος**.

Fuck me dude, that new Ducati is so boss.
Gha-mee-SEH mas, reh ma-LA-ka, EE-neh TZAH-meetoh toh keh-NOOR-yoh doo-KA-tee.
Γαμησέ μας, ρε μαλάκα, είναι **τζάμιτο** το καινούργιο Ντουκάτι.

Our cabbie was the shit. He got us there in no time.
Oh tah-REE-fahs mas EE-tahn MA-stoh-ras. Mas EH-feh-reh seh HROH-noh deh-TEH.
Ο ταρίφας μας ήταν **μάστορας**. Μας έφερε σε χρόνο ντε τε.

My professor is all right. He let me pass even though I failed the final.
EE-neh en-DA-ksee oh ka-thee-yee-TEES moo. Meh PE-ra-se par-OH-loh poo then EH-yra-psa stees eh-kse-TA-sees.
Είναι **εντάξει** ο καθηγητής μου. Με πέρασε, παρόλο που δεν έγραψα στις εξετάσεις.

THE BAD AND THE UGLY...

That **loser** hits on me every time he sees me.
*Af-TOHS oh **spa-SEE-klahs** moo teen pef-TEE KA-theh foh-RA poo meh VLEH-pee.*
Αυτός ο **σπασίκλας** μου την πέφτει κάθε φορά που με βλέπει.

That **hick** has no idea how we do things in the city.
*Af-TOS oh **VLA-hos** den EH-hee ee-THE-ah pos EH-hoon ta PRA-gma-tah steen POH-lee.*
Αυτός ο **βλάχος** δεν έχει ιδέα πώς έχουν τα πράγματα στην πόλη.

That **piece of shit** can go fuck himself.
*Na PAH-ee na gha-MEE-thee toh **ka-THEE-kee**.*
Να πάει να γαμηθεί το **καθίκι**.

Nobody here has any time for **mama's boys**.
*Ka-NEES eh-THOH then EH-hee OH-ra yia **BOO-lee-thes**.*
Κανείς εδώ δεν έχει ώρα για **μπούληδες**.

Did anybody else see what that **idiot** just did?
*EE-the ka-NEES AH-los tee EH-ka-neh oh **ee-LEE-thee-os**?*
Είδε κανείς άλλος τι έκανε ο **ηλίθιος**;

My little brother is such a **fatass**.
*Oh mee-KROS moo ah-ther-FOS EE-neh po-LEE **la-PAS**.*
Ο μικρός μου αδερφός είναι πολύ **λαπάς**.

That **ugly chick** would not leave me alone all night.
*Af-TOH toh **BAH-zo** then meh AH-fee-neh EE-see-ho OH-lo toh VRA-thee.*
Αυτό το **μπάζο** δεν με άφηνε ήσυχο όλο το βράδυ.

That **old hag** hit me with her cane.
*Meh VA-reh-seh meh to ba-stoo-nee tees ee **ko-LO-yhree-ah**.*
Με βάρεσε με το μπαστούνι της η **κωλόγρια**.

That **dirty old man** felt me up!
*Meh hoo-fto-seh oh **por-NO-yhe-ros**!*
Με χούφτωσε ο **πορνόγερος**!

Don't tell my mom anything, she is the biggest **gossip** I know.
*Meen pees Tee-poh-tah stee MAH-nah moo, EE-neh ee pyoh meh-GHAH-lee **koo-tsoh-BOH-la** poo KSEH-roh.*
Μην πεις τίποτα στη μάνα μου. Είναι η πιο μεγάλη **κουτσομπόλα** που ξέρω.

This latest generation is full of **slackers** and **stoners**.
*Af-TEE ee teh-lehf-TEH-ah yen-YAH ee-NEH yeh-MA-tee **teh-BEHL-ee-thes** keh **bahf-YAHR-ee-thes**.*
Αυτή η τελευταία γενιά είναι γεμάτη **τεμπέληδες** και **μπαφιάρηδες**.

Careful in this neighborhood, its full of thugs.
PROH-she-heh saf-TEEN tee yee-toh-NYA, EE-neh yeh-MAH-tee ah-LEE-tehs.
Πρόσεχε σ'αυτήντη γειτονιά, είναι γεμάτη **αλήτες**.

My sister keeps dating some freaks.
Ee ah-thehr-fee moo see-neh-HEE-zee nah VYEH-nee meh psee-HAH-kee-thehs.
Η αδερφή μου συνεχίζει να βγαίνει με **ψυχάκηδες**.

Why are you hanging around with fuck-ups?
Yah-TEE KAH-nees pah-REH-ah meh hah-MEH-noos?
Γιατί κάνεις παρέα με **χαμένους**;

Go change, you look like a bum.
PEE-yeh-neh AH-lah-kseh, FEH-neh-seh sahn YEE-ftohs.
Πήγαινε άλλαξε, φαίνεσαι σαν **γύφτος**.

Are you really going to bring that slut to Christmas dinner?
Soh-vah-RAH thah FEH-rees teen poo-TAH-nah stoh hrees-too-yen-AH-tee-koh trah-PE-zee?
Σοβαρά θα φέρεις την **πουτάνα** στο χριστουγεννιάτικο τραπέζι;

Shut up, you're unbearable!
SKA-seh, reh, then pa-LEH-veH-seh!
Σκάσε, ρε, **δεν παλεύεσαι**!

Please don't invite your cousin. He's really annoying when he's drunk.
Seh pa-ra-ka-LOH meen ka-LEH-sees tohn xah-thehr-FOH soo. EE-neh poh-LEE spahs-TEE-kohs OH-tahn PEE-nee.
Σε παρακαλώ μην καλέσεις τον ξαδερφό σου. Είναι πολύ **σπαστικός** όταν πίνει.

All the girls from the north burbs act super trendy with all their Gucci.
*OH-la tah kohr-EE-tsya AHP-tah voo-POO toh PEH-zoon poh-LEE **TREN-dee** meh tah GOO-tsee toos.*
Όλα τα κορίτσια απ' τα ΒΠ το παίζουν πολύ **τρέντι** με τα Γκούτσι τους.

All the rich kids live in the northern suburbs of Athens. They're so uniformly obnoxious that they've developed into their own little subculture.

I'm the unluckiest person in the world.
*EE-meh oh pio meh-YHA-lohs **ga-DEH-mees** stohn KOZ-moh.*
Είμαι ο πιο μεγάλος **γκαντέμης** στον κόσμο.

You're nuts!
*EE-seh **moor-LOHS**!*
Είσαι **μουρλός**!

He lost his mind.
EH-pa-theh psee-hee-KO trah-la-LA.
Έπαθε ψυχικό τραλαλά.

All politicians are so sleezy, it makes me nauseous.
*OH-lee ee poh-lee-tee-KEE EE-neh TOH-soh **ylee-OH-thehs**, poo THEH-lo na KA-no eh-meh-TO.*
Όλοι οι πολιτικοί είναι τόσο **γλοιώδεις**, που θέλω να κάνω εμετό.

Come on now, don't shit a shitter.
*EH-la TOH-ra, **steen poo-TA-na poo-ta-NIES**?*
Έλα τώρα, **στην πουτάνα πουτανιές**;

Literally, "Are you trying to con a whore?" You use this when someone tries to deceive someone who is good at deceiving people.

CHAPTER 3

PARTY GREEK
EH-LEE-NEE-KAH TEES
DEE-AH-SKEH-DAH-SEES
Ελληνικά της Διασκέδασης

It's not so much that Greeks go out a lot, it's that they barely ever go in. Whether it's food and coffee during the day or bars and clubs at night, nobody will show you how to spend a tax refund better than a Greek. First of all, no one goes for coffee like these people do — they do it better, harder, and longer than anyone else. As for the night life…you'd better drink a Red Bull, because it starts at midnight and doesn't end until you're in pain and late for work. And be prepared for a lesson in national pride, because at five in the morning, the Greek music drops. It doesn't matter what the DJ's been spinning all night, when the mood is right and the crowd is nice and liquored up, the old-school Greek beats hit the amplifiers and everybody sings — well, slurs — along.

····Let's go out tonight!
PA-meh EH-xoh ah-POH-pseh!
Πάμε έξω απόψε!

Let's party!
EH-la na VHOO-meh toh VRA-thee!
Έλα να βγούμε το βράδυ!

We're going out tonight.
***Thah VGOO-meh** ah-PO-pse.*
Θα βγούμε απόψε.

What does the night have in store?
***Tee PEH-zee** giah toh VRA-thee?*
Τι παίζει για το βράδυ;

Do you have any plans for tonight?
***EH-hees ka-no-NEE-see** yia ah-PO-pse?*
Έχεις κανονίσει για απόψε;

Let's go…
PA-meh na…
Πάμε να…

> **get a drink.**
> *PYOO-meh EH-na poh-TOH.*
> πιούμε ένα ποτό.

> **to the movies.**
> *see-neh-MA.*
> σινεμά.

> **clubbing**
> *KLA-beeng.*
> κλάμπινγκ.
> They do this A LOT.

Come on, let's go somewhere.
*EH-la na **PA-meh KA-poo**.*
Έλα να πάμε κάπου.

Are you hungry? Let's go eat.
Pee-NAS? PA-meh na FA-meh.
Πεινάς; Πάμε να φάμε.

I'm bored, let's go get a drink.
Var-YEH-meh, PA-meh na PYOO-meh EH-na po-TO.
Βαριέμαι, πάμε να πιούμε ένα ποτό.

Let's go grab a cup of coffee.
EH-la na PYOO-meh EH-nan ka-FE.
Έλα να πιούμε έναν καφέ.

A little more personal than just saying "coffee?" (καφέ;). Use this one when you're asking a girl you like.

I don't think we're going anywhere tonight.
*Then noh-MEE-zoh oh-TEE thah PAH-meh **poo-theh-NA** ah-PO-pseh.*
Δεν νομίζω ότι θα πάμε **πουθενά** απόψε.

I'm dead tired. There's no way I'm going out.
*EE-meh **koh-MA-tya**. Then PEH-zee na vgo.*
Είμαι **κομμάτια**. Δεν παίζει να βγω.

One drink and I'm out of here.
*EH-na po-TOH keh **teen KA-noh**.*
Ένα ποτό και **την κάνω**.

Couch and Internet tonight dude.
Ka-na-PEH keh EE-nter-net ah-PO-pse, FEE-leh.
Καναπέ και ίντερνετ απόψε, φίλε.

I'm chilling at home with my girlfriend tonight.
***Thah-RA-ksoh** SPEE-tee meh teen koh-PEH-la moo ah-PO-pseh.*
Θ' **αράξω** σπίτι με την κοπέλα μου απόψε.

Let's go…
PAH-meh…
Πάμε…

> **drinking.**
> *na ta PIOO-meh.*
> να τα πιούμε.

> **have a few.**
> *na ta TSOO-ksoo-meh.*
> να τα τσούξουμε.

clink our glasses.
na ta tsoo-GREE-soo-meh.
να τα τσουγκρίσουμε.

get drunk.
na meh-THEE-soo-meh.
να μεθύσουμε.

get shitfaced.
na YEE-noo-meh ska-TA.
να γίνουμε σκατά.

get fucked up.
na YEE-noo-meh HA-lia.
να γίνουμε χάλια.

get crazy.
na ta SPA-soo-meh.
να τα σπάσουμε.

····Where to go
Poo na PAS
Πού να πας

There's always somewhere to go, there's always something
to do. You'll soon find yourself going home only to shower and
you'll hate every minute you're there. At night, your options are
literally endless. There are breathtaking clubs on the beach
and trippy trance warehouses downtown. If you don't want
to go home bleeding from the ears, you're covered with 31
flavors of bar to choose from. Rock bars, Irish pubs, trendy
spots, dirty dives, beer gardens, and everything in between—
just pick your poison.

The bar
Toh bahr
Το μπαρ
From chic vodka bars to filthy gin mills to everything in between,
Athens has a bitchin' selection of watering holes in which to
drown your sorrows.

Ouzo bar
Oo-zeh-REE
Ουζερί

The Germans have beer gardens, the Irish have pubs, and the Greeks have ouzo shacks. They're a really chill alternative to the usual hang out spots.

Nightclub
Klab/kla-BA-kee
Κλαμπ/κλαμπάκι

By far the most popular nighttime option, the clubs in Greece are fuckin' amazing. They're big and grand, the techno is slapping, the dancers are hot, and the bouncers can kill you. Miami and LA ain't got shit on Athens.

Greek nightclub
Skee-LA-thee-ko
Σκυλάδικο

Usually, you get sent to the dog house when you fuck up and say the wrong name in bed. In Greece, you go to the doghouse to meet some new names. A σκυλάδικο, which literally means "doghouse," is a Greek music club. If you're not in the mood for techno and you want to hear some local talent, make your way to one of these. The atmosphere is always good and there's a lot of drinking and dancing going on.

Greek blues club
Reh-beh-TA-thee-ko
Ρεμπετάδικο

Ρεμπέτικα (*reh-BEH-tee-ka*) is traditional Greek music that talks about the pain of the people. It's bluesy and soulful, and the bouzouki solos are bitchin'. A ρεμπετάδικο is a smoke-filled hole in the wall, usually in a sketchy part of town. You always have a good, wine-saturated time here.

Beer hall
Bee-ra-REE-ah
Μπιραρία

They sell beer by the meter here. How cool is that!? Usually German-themed, you can get a wide variety of ice-cold Bavarian brews and tons of greasy food to wash them down with.

Movie theater
See-neh-MA
Σινεμά

If you aren't in the mood to wake up hungover and full of regrets, you can take it easy and catch a flick. Fortunately, they use subtitles and don't dub the movies here.

Concert
See-na-VLEE-ah
Συναυλία

There are always at least a few concerts going on, and you can usually take your pick of genre, from Greek to techno to rock and everything in between. There are lots of great outdoor concerts during the summer too.

House party
HA-ooz PAR-tee
Χάουζ πάρτι

Titty bar
Ko-LO-ba-ro
Κωλόμπαρο

Technically called an "ass bar" in Greek, but hey, same difference.

The square
Pla-TEE-ah
Πλατεία

The equivalent of brown bagging it on your front porch, every neighborhood has a square where you can have a good night on the cheap. Just buy a six pack of Heineken and some Smirnoff Ice for the ladies from one of the 24-hour kiosks and you're good. You'll also have live entertainment from the skaters, stoners, and emos that frequent these spots.

Street races
KOHN-dres
Κόντρες

Greek cop cars are slooowww, dude. If you have 200 horses and at least some skill, you can get away. That's probably why this pasttime is still going strong. Go hang out, watch the races, or join in if you're so inclined. The music's loud and there's usually a food truck nearby, so the beer's cold and the food's good too.

County fair
Pa-nee-YEE-ree
Πανηγύρι

Make sure you get yourself some spit-roasted lamb when you go to these.

Carnival
Kar-na-VAL
Καρναβάλι

These Brazilian-themed street parties are held in every major city during the carnival period—about 60 days before Easter, it lasts three weeks—and there's always a lot of debauchery and samba going on. The biggest and craziest carnival takes place in the city of Patras, in Peloponnesus.

THE BOOZE)))

ΤΑ ΞΙΔΙΑ

Beer
BEE-ra
Μπίρα

Greece would traditionally be considered a wine-drinking culture, but beer is definitely not a shunned or unpopular choice. You may hear it called the diminutive μπιρίτσα (*bee-REE-tsa*) or the more juvenile μπιρόνι (*bee-ROH-nee*).

Red / white **wine**
*KO-kee-no / lef-KO **kra-SEE***
Κόκκινο / λευκό **κρασί**

Rosé wine
Ro-ZEH kra-SEE
Ροζέ κρασί

Very popular in Greece. This wine goes exceptionally well with anything that is grilled. Just make sure it's nice and cold.

Barrel wine
Kra-SEE HEE-ma
Κρασί χύμα

Χύμα means unfiltered or in your face, both physically and conceptually. In this case, it refers to wines that are not bottled at a winery. They are poured in into pitchers straight from the barrel and sipped from big shot glasses. The ρεμπετάδικα and the ταβέρνες serve this kind exclusively.

Retsina
Reh-TSEE-na
Ρετσίνα

Retsina is a traditional white, resinated wine. It's been fucking people up since ancient times.

Ouzo
OO-zo
Ούζο
The classic Greek liquor made from aniseed. It has a mild licorice taste and goes great with olives, cucumber, and feta.

Tsipouro
TSEE-poo-roh
Τσίπουρο
This is the moonshine. It's a pomace brandy, and it is STRONG (40–45% alcohol). You'll get the best stuff from the rednecks in the villages.

Raki
Rah-KEE
Ρακί
Tsipouro is from the island of Crete. Raki is pretty much the same stuff, just don't tell that to a Cretan.

Whiskey
WEE-skee
Ουίσκι

Vodka
VOT-ka
Βότκα

Tequila
Teh-KEE-la
Τεκίλα
Mainly drunk as a shot. Most places only have José, so be prepared.

Bailey's
BAY-leez
Μπέιλιζ
Very popular in coffee, most notably in the Bailey's **Φραπέ** (frappé) incarnation, which is one of the best liquid hangover cures ever invented.

····Cheers
YA-mas
Γεια μας

Just like in any other place, Greeks clink their glasses. One distinction to keep in mind is that you never cheers with water or coffee, not even as a joke. It's very bad luck.

Can I get a **shot** of tequila please?
*Boh-ROH nah EH-ho EH-nah **sfee-NA-kee** the-KEE-la, pah-rah-ka-LOH?*
Μπορώ να έχω ένα **σφηνάκι** τεκίλα, παρακαλώ;
You'll most likely be exclusively using the plural form, σφηνάκια (*sfee-NAH-kya*).

Man, this is some **bad booze**.
*Ma-LA-ka, ah-FTO EE-neh **bO-ba**.*
Μαλάκα, αυτό είναι **μπόμπα**.
Cheap or spiked booze. Some of the shadier clubs refill their empty bottles with cheap, no-name alcohol. This shit will give you the most ultimate of hangovers.

I could really use a **drink** right now.
*Tha EE-theh-lah EH-nah **po-TOH** TOH-rah.*
Θα ήθελα ένα **ποτό** τώρα.

Should we get a **bottle** of wine?
*Na htee-PEE-soo-meh EH-nah **boo-KA-lee** krah-SEE?*
Να χτυπήσουμε ένα **μπουκάλι** κρασί;

I'll have a **glass** of the rosé.
*Tha PAH-roh EH-na **poh-TEE-ree** ro-ZEH.*
Θα πάρω ένα **ποτήρι** ροζέ.

To our health!
Steen ee-YA mas!
Στην υγειά μας!

This is the official way of saying cheers in Greece.

Cheers!
YA mas!
Γεια μας!

Cheers to us and to our big dicks.
YA-mas, sta ma-kree-AH poo-LYA mas.
Γεια μας, στα μακριά πουλιά μας.
For the guys.

Cheers to us and to our big tits.
YA-mas, sta meh-GHA-la veez-YA mas.
Γεια μας, στα μεγάλα βυζιά μας.
For the ladies.

Come on, drink up!
*AH-deh, **AH-sprohs PA-tohs**!*
Άντε, **άσπρος πάτος**!
Loosely translates to "empty glass."

••••Drunk
Meh-theez-MEH-nohs
Μεθυσμένος

I've drunk...
EH-hoh py-EE...
Έχω πιει...

> **a lot.**
> *po-LEE.*
> πολύ.
>
> **everything.**
> *ton ah-YLEH-oh-ra.*
> τον αγλέορα.
>
> **my ass off.**
> *tohn KOH-loh moo.*
> τον κώλο μου.
>
> **my head off.**
> *ta ke-ra-TA moo.*
> τα κέρατά μου.
> Literally, "my horns off."

I'm...
EE-meh...
Είμαι...

tipsy.
psee-loh-zah-lee-ZMEH-nos.
ψιλοζαλισμένος.

drunk.
meh-theez-MEH-nohs.
μεθυσμένος.

shitfaced.
skah-TA.
σκατά.

a mess.
HAL-ya.
χάλια.

wasted.
gol.
γκολ.

sloppy drunk.
LYOH-ma.
λιώμα.

trashed.
PEE-ta.
πίτα.
Literally, "pie."

blind drunk.
TEE-fla stoh meh-THEE-see.
τύφλα στο μεθύσι.

fucked up.
GHA-mee-SE-ta.
γάμησέ τα.

gone.
ko-MA-tya.
κομμάτια.
Literally, "in pieces," this word is used for "drunk" and for "dead tired/out of it." It's very popular and used frequently for both meanings.

····The morning after

Toh eh-PO-meh-no proh-EE
Το επόμενο πρωί

Dude, I don't remember anything from last night.
Ma-LA-ka, then thee-MA-meh TEE-poh-ta ah-PO hthes.
Μαλάκα, δεν θυμάμαι τίποτα από χθες.

I have a crazy hangover.
*EH-hoh treh-LOH **poh-noh-KEH-fa-loh**.*
Έχ ω τρελό **πονοκέφαλο**.
Literally, "headache." There's no actual word for "hangover" in Greek.

I might've had a few too many.
Noh-MEE-zoh pos EE-pya LEE-ghoh pa-ra-PA-noh.
Νομίζω πως ήπια λίγο παραπάνω.

I got fucked up last night.
Ga-MEE-thee-ka hthes toh VRA-thee.
Γαμήθηκα χθες το βράδυ.

I think we overdid it last night at the club.
***Toh pah-ra-KA-na-meh** hthes stoh klab.*
Το παρακάναμε χθες στο κλαμπ.

I'm never drinking again.
Then xa-na-PEE-noh po-TEH.
Δεν ξαναπίνω ποτέ.

Dude, what did we do last night?
Ma-LA-ka, tee KA-na-meh hthes toh VRA-thee?
Μαλάκα, τι κάναμε χθες το βράδυ;
Can also be asked rhetorically to express amazement at the craziness and debauchery that went down last night.

····Weed
FOO-da
Φούντα

It may be ranked as a class-A drug, but that doesn't really stop the people from burning. Weed has been part of the Greek culture for quite some time. The old school Greek blues (ρεμπέτικο) musicians famously smoked hashish before they would pick up their instruments; you can hear the hookah bubbling in the background on many old vinyl recordings. Today, you can find weed fairly easily throughout Athens. Just ask your friends, and someone will know someone who knows someone.

Let's go smoke a joint.
*PA-meh na **PYOO-meh EH-na tsee-GA-ro**.*
Πάμε να **πιούμε ένα τσιγάρο**.
The word τσιγάρο means "cigarette," but the word πιούμε means "drink," and this combination of drinking a cigarette implies weed. Τσιγάρο is often shortened to γάρο (GHA-ro).

Hash
Ha-SEE-see
Χασίσι

Weed
FOO-da
Φούντα
You might hear this shortened to φου (foo) sometimes.

Skunk
Skahnk
Σκανκ
This is the good shit.

Grass
HOHR-toh
Χόρτο
A little old-fashioned, like something your parents would say.

Green
PRA-see-noh
Πράσινο

Joint
BAH-fos
Μπάφος

Why don't you pass that joint over this way?
*Yah PA-sa-reh ton **BAH-foh** AH-poh-thoh.*
Για πάσαρε τον **μπάφο** από 'δώ.

Dude, roll a joint, I've had a shit day.
*Ma-LA-ka, **STREE-pse EH-na tsee-GHA-roh**, EE-hah ska-TA MEH-ra.*
Μαλάκα, **στρίψε ένα τσιγάρο**, είχα σκατά μέρα.

Do you smoke?
PEE-nees?
Πίνεις;
This phrase is very contextual, since you're really asking, "Do you drink?" Use it only if you're in some sort of herbal situation.

····Drugs
Nar-ko-tee-KA
Ναρκωτικά

There's a bit of a drug culture in Greece, mainly because of the summer party scene. It's not Studio 54, but you can pretty much get your hands on any pill or powder you'd like. Careful though, because you will be royally fucked if the cops decide to do their job.

Do you have any…?
EH-hees kah-THOH-loo…?
Έχεις καθόλου..;

> **cocaine**
> *koh-ka-EE-nee*
> κοκαΐνη

> **coke**
> *koh-ka/koh-koh*
> κόκα/κοκό

>> **One line of coke and I'm good to go all night.**
>> *MEE-ah ghra-mee **KOH-ka** keh EE-meh set OH-loh toh VRA-thee.*
>> Μια γραμμή **κόκα** και είμαι σετ όλο το βράδυ.

> **heroine**
> *ee-roh-EE-nee*
> ηρωίνη

> **pill/pills**
> *koo-BEE/koo-BYA*
> κουμπί/κουμπιά

> **smack**
> *PREH-za*
> πρέζα

> **Ecstasy**
> *EK-sta-see*
> Έκστασι

> **E**
> *EH-psee-lohn*
> Έψιλον

> **acid**
> *el-es-DEE*
> LSD

> **mushrooms**
> *ma-nee-TAR-ya*
> μανιτάρια

····High
Ma-STOO-ra
Μαστούρα

I'm stoned.
EE-meh klahs-MEH-nos.
κλασμένος.

Literally, "I'm farted." It sounds weird in English, but this is actually one of the more common ways of saying you're stoned.

I'm high off my ass.
EH-hoh heh-STEE.
Έχω χεστεί.

Literally, "I've shat myself." Again, much like κλάσμενος, this sounds weird in English, but it's frequently used.

Dude, **I'm stoned out of my mind.**
*Ma-LA-ka, **teen EH-hohah-KOO-see**.*
Μαλάκα, **την έχω ακούσει**.

I'm gone.
EE-meh koh-MA-tya
Είμαι κομμάτια

You've probably noticed how liberally this word is used. This is its third incarnation, after "tired" and "drunk".

I'm loaded.
EE-meh TOOR-boh.
Είμαι τούρμπο.

One of my personal favorites.

I'm faded.
Then ee-PAR-ho.
Δεν υπάρχω.

Literally, "I don't exist." You know when you're so high that you're just not in your body anymore? No? That's good, but if you do, then you have a good idea of how and when to drop this one.

Dude, Elvis has left the building.
FEE-leh, then ee-PAR-hoh af-TEEN tee steeg-MEE.
Φίλε, δεν υπάρχω αυτήν τη στιγμή.

I'm burned out.
EH-hoh ka-EE/EH-hoh KA-psee.
Εχω καεί/έχω κάψει.

You are such a…
EE-seh TOH-soh…
Είσαι τόσο…

> **burnout.**
> *ka-MEH-nohs.*
> καμένος.

> **pot head.**
> *ha-see-KLEES / ha-see-KLOO .*
> χασικλής / χασικλού.

> **stoner.**
> *bahf-YAH-rees.*
> μπαφιάρης.

> **coke head.**
> *koh-KA-kias.*
> κοκάκιας.

> **heroine addict.**
> *preh-ZOH-nee.*
> πρεζόνι.

I'm quitting cold turkey.
Thah toh KOH-psoh ma-HEH-ree.
Θα το κόψω μαχαίρι.

I'm clean.
EE-meh ka-tha-ROS.
Είμαι καθαρός.

Detox
Ah-poh-toh-XEE-noh-see
Αποτοξίνωση

His parents sent him to rehab in Spain.
*Ee ghoh-NEES too tohn STEE-la-neh seh **KEH-droh ah-poh-toh-KSEE-noh-sees** steen Ee-spa-NEE-ah.*
Οι γονείς του τον στείλανε σε **κέντρο αποτοξίνωσης** στην Ισπανία.

····Five-O
BAH-tsee
Μπάτσοι

Greeks in general don't like or respect the police. They either see them as fascist pigs, or lazy good-for-nothing guys with small-penis syndrome. This sentiment goes hand in hand with the blatant disregard for many laws that are considered to result in victimless crimes if and when they are broken.

Cop
BAH-tsohs
Μπάτσος

Oh shit, **the cops!**
*Poh, reh POO-stee, ee **ba-tsa-REE-ah!***
Πώ, ρε πούστη, η **μπατσαρία**!
Not necessarily two or more cops.

The pigs
Ghoo-ROO-nya
Γουρούνια

Cop car
Ba-tsee-KOH
Μπατσικό
Another popular way to refer to a cop car is μποκσεράκι (*boh-kser-AH-kee*), literally "boxer shorts." The logic behind this is that just like a pair of boxers, there's a dick inside.

Cops on bikes
Zee-TAS
Ζητάς
These guys specialize in stopping street racing, and speeding in general. They have fast motorbikes that they use to pose as fellow boy racers in order to egg you on and then ruin your night. The only way to distinguish them is from the "Z" badge on their helmets, which of course you can't see when they pull up behind you and rev their engines.

Undercover cop
Ah-sfah-LEE-tees
Ασφαλίτης
The undercover police force is called "Ασφάλεια" (*Ah-SFAH-lee-ah*).

Police van
KLOO-va
Κλούβα
This is what they throw you into when you're drunk and belligerent in public. You know, a paddy wagon.

Riot police
Maht
Ματ
You'll see these guys a lot at soccer games. They're the ones in green uniforms and they can beat the shit out you during the demonstrations.

Jail
Fee-la-KEE
Φυλακή

Jail cell
Keh-LEE
Κελί
Here's hoping your night doesn't end up here.

CHAPTER 4

BODY GREEK
EH-LEE-NEE-KAH GIA TOH SOH-MAH
Ελληνικά για το σώμα

Naked statues, greased-up wrestlers, loose-fitting togas, and the movie 300. It's obvious that from day one the Greeks haven't had much of a problem showing some skin. Just like in every other country but the U.S., the people tend to be in good shape. We're talking about a hot and sunny place with tons of beaches, so if you don't look good naked, you're going to be at a disadvantage. On the other hand, Greeks love to chill and have a good time, so there are also some love handles flapping about. Just make sure you're not super-fucking pale during the summer or you'll stick out like a sore thumb against the backdrop of olive skin that dominates the scene.

····Damn he's sexy
EE-neh SEH-xee
Είναι σέξι

True beauty is in the details, and what better way to express your appreciation of someone's details than to have a vocab chockfull of, well…detail?

Did you see the **arms** on that **stud**?
*EE-thes tee **BRA-tsa** poo EH-hee af-TOH toh **pe-THEE**?*
Είδες τι **μπράτσα** που έχει αυτό το **παιδί**;

Παιδί means "kid," but it can imply different versions of kids depending on the situation. "The kid needs to go to bed" and "that kid wrecked me last night" are two different things entirely.

I'm a sucker for a good set of **abs**.
*EH-hoh ah-THEE-na-MEE-ah stoos **kee-lee-ah-KOOS**.*
Έχω αδυναμία στους **κοιλιακούς**.

I'm going to the gym to **get ripped**, but I'm making sure I don't **bulk up**.
*PA-oh yee-mna-STEE-ree-oh yia na **ghrah-MOH-soh**, ah-LA proh-SEH-hoh na mee **VAH-loh OH-gho**.*
Πάω γυμναστήριο για να **γραμμώσω**, αλλά προσέχω να μη **βάλω όγκο**.

I like my guy to be **strong** and **solid**.
*Moo ah-REH-see oh AHN-dras na EE-neh **thee-na-TOHS** keh **yeh-roh-theh-MEH-nohs**.*
Μου αρέσει ο άνδρας να είναι **δυνατός** και **γεροδεμένος**.

Am I right, ladies?

Hey, my mama says I'm **handsome**!
*Eh, EE MA-na moo LEH-ee pohs EE-meh **ah-reh-noh-POHS**!*
Εε, η μάνα μου λέει πως είμαι **αρρενωπός**!

Damn girl, your new boy toy is **gorgeous**!
*Ka-LA moh-REE, **KOOK-lohs** toh keh-NOOR-yoh ah-MOHR-eh!*
Καλά, μωρή, **κούκλος** το καινούργιο αμόρε!

You're lucky you have a **chest** like that.
*EH-heh HA-ree poo EH-hees TEH-tyo **STEE-thohs**.*
Έχε χάρη που έχεις τέτοιο **στήθος**.

Most guys don't know how to work out their **calves**.
*Ee pyo poh-LEE AHN-dres then yee-MNA-zoon tees **GHA-behs** toos sohs-TA.*
Οι πιο πολλοί άνδρες δεν γυμνάζουν τις **γάμπες** τους σωστά.

What's a nice **back** gonna do if it's covered with **zits**?
*Tee nah soo KA-nee ee oh-REH-ah **PLA-tee** AH-ma EE-neh yeh-MA-tee **bee-BEE-kya**?*
Τι να σου κάνει η ωραία **πλάτη** άμα είναι γεμάτη **μπιμπίκια**;

If you go to Greece during the summer, you'll undoubtedly be spending a good deal of time with your shirt off, so good skin is important. Thankfully, the sea water does wonders for the epidermis.

Dude, what can I say, it's my **jawline**. It opens doors.
*Ma-LA-ka, tee na soo poh, FTEH-ee toh **sa-GHO-nee** moo. Ah-NEE-yee POR-tes.*
Μαλάκα, τι να σου πω, φταίει το **σαγόνι** μου. Ανοίγει πόρτες.

····Sexy mama
Kah-FTEE GOH-meh-nah
Καυτή γκόμενα

All three of the following expressions for hotness revolve around the word μουνί, which means, well, pussy. But keep your pants zipped, there'll be more in the next chapter. The important thing to keep in mind here is that, even though they may sound a little crass, these phrases are the most common ways of referring to a particularly attractive member of the fairer sex.

Dude, she's...
Φίλε, είναι...
FEE-leh EE-neh...

> **hot.**
> *moo-NA-ra.*
> μουνάρα.

> **crazy hot.**
> *treh-LOH moo-NEE.*
> τρελό μουνί.

> **fucking hot.**
> *gha-MOH ta moo-NYA.*
> γαμώ τα μουνιά.

> **fine.**
> *MOO-na-rohs.*
> μούναρος.

Careful you don't lose this one, you idiot, she's just so adorable.
PROH-she-heh meen tee HA-sees af-TEEN ka-koh-MEE-ree moo, EE-neh TOH-soh seem-pa-thee-tee-KEE.
Πρόσεχε μην τη χάσεις αυτήν κακομοίρη μου, είναι τόσο **συμπαθητική**.
Raise your hand if you've heard this phrase uttered to you before from your friends or family.

It's impossible how **cute** you are.
*Then YEE-neh-teh na EE-seh TOH-soh **ylee-KYA**.*
Δεν γίνεται να είσαι τόσο **γλυκιά**.

Fuck me, dude, look at that **gorgeous** girl!
*Poh, reh POOS-tee moo, KEE-ta af-TOH toh **koo-KLEE**!*
Πω, ρε πούστη μου, κοίτα αυτό το **κουκλί**!

You're really **pretty**.
*EE-seh **po-LEE OH-mor-fee**.*
Είσαι **πολύ όμορφη**.

That girl is **giving me a semi**.
***SKE-tee KAV-la** ee GOH-meh-na.*
Σκέτη καύλα η γκόμενα.

This is a very popular expression.

It's easy to talk shit about our dry spells when you're
hanging out with that **supermodel** of yours.
*EE-neh EF-koh-loh na less ma-la-KEE-es yia tees ah-gha-
MEE-es mas OH-tahn teen **theh-oh-GOH-meh-na**.*
Είναι εύκολο να λες μαλακίες για τις αγαμίες μας, όταν
κυκλοφορείς με την **θεογκόμενα**.

I don't know how else to tell you this, but you have
ridiculously **slamming body**.
*Then XEH-roh pohs na stoh poh, ah-LA EH-hees **ke gha-
MO ta SOH-ma-ta**.*
Δεν ξέρω πως να στο πω, αλλά έχεις **και γαμώ τα
σώματα**.

She's got **legs for days**.
*EH-hee **PO-thya ah-teh-LEE-oh-ta**.*
Έχει **πόδια ατελείωτα**.

The word πόδια is used for both "legs" and "feet." There are
specific words for calves (γάμπες), thighs (μπούτια), and ankles
(αστράγαλος), but use πόδια if you're just trying to say legs.

Jesus Christ, her ass is **driving me fucking crazy**.
***Meh treh-LEH-nee** toh koh-LEE tees, gha-moh tohn
hree-STOH moo.*
Με τρελαίνει το κωλί της, γαμώ τον Χριστό μου.

It's over if she doesn't have a nice waist and hips.
*Meh ha-LA-ee AH-ma then PEH-zee **MEH-see** keh ka-THOH-loo **ghoh-FEE**.*
Με χαλάει άμα δεν παίζει καλή **μέση** και καθόλου **γοφοί**.

And the best part, flat stomach and zero cellulite!
*Keh toh ka-LEE-teh-roh, **stoh-MA-hee PLAh-kah**keh**kee-ta-REE-tee-tha** mee-THEN!*
Και το καλύτερο, **στομάχι πλάκα** και **κυτταρίτιδα** μηδέν!

····Not so hot
LEE-gho HAHL-ya
Λίγο χάλια

That bitch is fugly.
***BA-zoh** ee GOH-meh-na.*
Μπάζο η γκόμενα.

This is a really popular way of saying that she might actually have to be smart to get by. Use the word μπάζο as a default if you're not too sure what else might be appropriate.

For sure, dude, nice body, but come on now, she's a butter face.
*STAH-dahr reh ka-LOH SOH-ma ah-LA, EH-hee **skee-LOH-fa-tsa**.*
Στάνταρ, ρε καλό σώμα, αλλά, έλα τώρα, έχει **σκυλόφατσα**.

My god, he's hideous!
*Theh moo, EE-neh **ka-KAS-hee-mos**!*
Θεέ μου, είναι **κακάσχημος**!

I don't want to be mean, but she could stand to lose a few pounds.
*Then THEH-loh NA-meh ka-KOS ah-LA thah boh-ROO-she HA-see **KA-na kee-LOH**.*
Δεν θέλω να 'μαι κακός αλλά θα μπορούσε να χάσει **κάνα κιλό**.

Dude, he's a dwarf.
Ma-LA-ka, sah NA-nohs EE-neh.
Μαλάκα, σαν **νάνος** είναι.

Dude, she's not that big a deal.
See-YHA toh moo-NEE, reh ma-LA-ka.
Σιγά το μουνί, ρε μαλάκα.

Are you insane, that bitch is so not hot.
Treh-LA-thee-kess, reh, EE-neh FEH-ta ee kar-YOH-la.
Τρελάθηκες, ρε, είναι **φέτα** η καριόλα.
Yes, like the cheese.

She's awful.
HAL-ya ee GO-meh-na.
Χάλια η γκόμενα.

Why are you such a fatty?
Ya-TEE EE-seh TOH-soh hoh-droh-ba-LAS?
Γιατί είσαι τόσο **χοντρομπαλάς**;

Uuuhh, she's a bit piggy.
Eheh, EE-neh LEE-gho ghoo-ROO-na.
Εεε, είναι λίγο **γουρούνα**.

Look at the gut on that motherfucker.
KEE-ta MEE-ah BA-ka poo EH-hee oh POOS-tees.
Κοίτα μία **μπάκα** που έχει ο πούστης.

She's all right but she's got a major muffin top.
Ka-LEE EE-neh ah-LA EH-hee poh-LA pya-SEE-ma-ta.
Καλή είναι αλλά έχει πολλά **πιασίματα**.

Πιασίματα more accurately translates to "love handles," but that
seems to be more of a Dirty English issue than a Greek one.

He/She's...
Af-TOHS/Af-TEE EE-neh...
Αυτός/Αυτή είναι...

> **sloppy.**
> *tsa-pa-TSOO-lees/tsa-pa-TSOO-la.*
> τσαπατσούλης/τσαπατσούλα.

> **funny looking.**
> *peh-REE-er-ghos/peh-REE-er-yee.*
> Περίεργος/Περίεργη.

> **chubby.**
> *yeh-ma-TOO-lees/yeh-ma-TOO-la.*
> γεματούλης/γεματούλα.

> **formless.**
> *AH-mohr-fohs/AH-mohr-fee.*
> άμορφος/άμορφη.

> **boney.**
> *koh-Ka-LYA-rees/koh-ka-LYA-ra.*
> κοκαλιάρης/κοκαλιάρα.

> **anorexic.**
> *ah-noh-reh-xee-KOHS/ah-noh-reh-xee-KEE.*
> ανορεξικός/ανορεξική.

> **gap-toothed.**
> *stra-voh-THOH-dees/stra-voh-THOH-da.*
> στραβοδόντης/στραβοδόντα.

> **bow-legged.**
> *stra-voh-KA-nees/stra-voh-KA-na.*
> στραβοκάνης/στραβοκάνα.

> **cross-eyed.**
> *stra-voh-MA-tees/stra-voh-MA-ta.*
> στραβομάτης/στραβομάτα.

····The human body

Toh an-THRO-pee-no SOH-ma

Το ανθρώπινο σώμα

What's crackin' beanpole?

Tee YEE-neh-teh, reh psee-LEH?

Τι γίνεται, ρε **ψηλέ**;

He's way too short for me.

EE-neh po-LEE kon-DOHS yia MEH-na.

Είναι πολύ **κοντός** για μένα.

Eat something, you're way too skinny.

FA-eh KA-tee, EE-seh ee-per-vo-LEE-ka ah-THEE-na-tos.

Φάε κάτι, είσαι υπερβολικά **αδύνατος**.

Petite girls drive me crazy.

Meh treh-LEH-noo-neh ee mee-kro-ka-moh-MEH-ness.

Με τρελαίνουνε οι **μικροκαμωμένες**.

I'm not fat, I'm just big-boned!

Then EE-meh hohn-DROHS, EE-meh vah-ree-KOH-ka-lohs!

Δεν είμαι **χοντρός**, είμαι **βαρυκόκαλος**!

Yup, they have the exact same saying.

That fatass ate the last slice!

Eh-fa-YEH toh teh-lef-TEH-oh ko-MA-tee oh la-PAS!

Έφαγε το τελευταίο κομμάτι ο **λαπάς**!

She has such a cute face.

EH-hee po-LEE ylee-KEE FA-tsa.

Έχει πολύ γλυκιά **φάτσα**.

Look me in the eyes when you're talking to me, son.

KEE-ta meh sta MA-tya OH-tahn moo mee-LAS, mee-KREH.

Κοίτα με στα **μάτια** όταν μου μιλάς, μικρέ.

I don't think they make a helmet that'll fit your big-ass head.

*Then noh-MEE-zoh pohs ee-PAHR-hee KRAH-nohs poo thah hoh-REH see teen **keh-FA-la** soo.*

Δεν νομίζω πως υπάρχει κράνος που θα χωρέσει την **κεφάλα** σου.

Look at the schnozz on that dude.

*KEE-ta MEE-ah **mee-TOHN-ga** poo EH-hee oh tee-PAS.*

Κοίτα μία **μυτόγκα** που έχει ο τυπάς.

My teeth are yellow from all the smoking.

*Ta **THOH-dya** moo EE-neh KEE-tree-na AP-toh poh-LEE tsee-GHA-roh.*

Τα **δόντια** μου είναι κίτρινα απ' το πολύ τσιγάρο.

I'd tell you where to put those dick-sucking lips of yours, but there are children present.

*Thah SOO-leh-gha poo na VA-lees tah **tsee-boo-KOH-hee-la** soo, ah-LA ee-PAHR-xoo-neh peh-THYA.*

θα σού 'λεγα πού να βάλεις τα **τσιμπουκόχειλά** σου, αλλά υπάρχουνε παιδιά.

Time and a place for everything. Use χείλια (*HEE-lya*) if you just want to say "lips."

Let me get on your shoulders so I can see the stage.
*AH-seh meh na-neh-VOH stoos **OH-moos** soo yah na thoh teen skee-NEE.*
Άσε με ν' ανεβώ στους **ώμους** σου για να δω τη σκηνή.

My fingers are way too small for my hands.
*Tah **THAH-htee-la** moo EE-neh poh-LEE mee-KRA yia ta **HEHR-ya** moo.*
Τα **δάχτυλα** μου είναι πολύ μικρά για τα **χέρια** μου.
The problems some people have…

There isn't a girl left that hasn't pierced her belly button.
*Then EH-hee MEE-nee koh-REE-tsee poo then EH-hee KAH-nee PEER-seeng stohn **ah-fa-LOH**.*
Δεν έχει μείνει κορίτσι που δεν έχει κάνει πίρσινγκ στον **αφαλό**.
The word αφαλός comes from φάλλος, which is the Greek word for fallus. Α-φαλός literally means "above the fallus."

Dude, your feet stink!
*Ma-LA-ka, vroh-MA-neh ta **POTH-ya** soo!*
Μαλάκα, βρομάνε τα **πόδια** σου!

My boyfriend is hairy like a bear.
*Toh ah-GHO-ree moo EE-neh **tree-ho-TOHS** san ar-KOO-tha.*
Το αγόρι μου είναι **τριχωτός σαν αρκούδα**.

····Sleep
EE-pnos
Ύπνος

If you're here for the summer then you probably won't get much sleep at night. Get used to taking power naps on the beach…under the umbrella so you don't wake up looking like a rotisserie chicken.

I'm so tired.
*EE-meh po-LEE **koo-raz-MEH-nos**.*
Είμαι πολύ **κουρασμένος**.

Dude, I'm exhausted.
EE-meh ko-MA-tya, reh FEE-le.
Είμαι **κομμάτια,** ρε φίλε.

Κομμάτια means "pieces," so you're literally saying "I'm in pieces," or "I'm falling apart." This is by far the most popular way for youngsters and hipsters to express fatigue (or a hangover).

I can't stand up anymore.
Then bo-RO, tha PEH-so KA-toh.
Δεν μπορώ, θα πέσω κάτω.

I'm going to go lay down for a little bit.
PA-oh na xa-PLOH-soh yia LEE-gho.
Πάω να **ξαπλώσω** για λίγο.

I can't even focus my eyes.
Then VLE-poh broh-STA moo.
Δεν βλέπω μπροστά μου.

I went fucking overboard on the sleep.
Gha-MEE-thee-ka ston EE-pno.
Γαμήθηκα στον ύπνο.

I'm going to take a nap.
Tha REE-xoh EH-nan ee-PNA-koh.
Θα ρίξω έναν **υπνάκο**.

I'm going to hit the sack.
PA-oh na teen PEH-so.
Πάω να **την πέσω**.

I'm going to sleep.
PA-oh na kee-mee-THO.
Πάω να **κοιμηθώ**.

Sorry, I snore hella loud!
SOH-ree, roo-ha-LEE-zoh sahn POOS-tees!
Σόρι, **ροχαλίζω** σαν πούστης!

····The beach
EE pa-ra-LEE-ah
Η παραλία

Russians have their bathhouses, the Swedes have their masseuses, and the Greeks have their beaches. The country is a peninsula, and there are six THOUSAND islands large and small surrounding it. Only about 250 are inhabited, but that's still a hell of a lot of places to tan, swim, and be seen. So make sure you're in swimsuit shape, grab your sunscreen and your oversized sunglasses, and go soak up some of that Mediterranean sun before global warming turns Scotland into the new Tahiti.

This bathing suit doesn't look good on me at all.
*Then moo PA-ee ka-THOH-loo af-TOH toh **ma-YOH**.*
Δεν μού πάει καθόλου αυτό το **μαγιό**.

I'm going to take a dip to cool off.
*PA-oh na KA-noh MEE-ah **voo-TYA** na throh-see-STOH.*
Πάω να κάνω μία **βουτιά** να δροσιστώ.

The salt's good for your skin.
KA-nee ka-LOH stoh THER-ma toh ah-LA-tee.
Κάνει καλό στο δέρμα το αλάτι.
It really is.

He's in beach shape.
EH-hee KA-nee SOH-ma yia pa-ra-LEE-ah.
Έχει κάνει σώμα για παραλία.

Come on, let's go to the nude beach.
*EH-la na PA-meh steen **pa-ra-LEE-ah gee-mnee-STON**.*
Έλα να πάμε στην **παραλία γυμνιστών**.

The sand is burning my feet.
*Ee **AH-moh** moo KEH-ee tees pa-TOO-ses.*
Η **άμμος** μου καίει της πατούσες.

GETTING TANNED)))
MA-VREE-ZOH-DAS
ΜΑΥΡΙΖΟΝΤΑΣ

Put on some **sunscreen** before you burn.
*VA-leh LEE-gho **ah-dee-lee-ah-KO** preen ka-EES.*
Βάλε λίγο **αντηλιακό** πριν καείς.

I have to **get some color** before the summer's over.
*PREH-pee **na PA-roh LEE-gho HROH-ma** preen teh-lee-OH-see toh ka-loh-KE-ree.*
Πρέπει να **πάρω λίγο χρώμα** πριν τελειώσει το καλοκαίρι.

I'm **tanning topless** today.
*SEE-meh-ra tha KA-noh **TOP-les MAV-reez-ma**.*
Σήμερα θα κάνω **τόπλες μαύρισμα**.

You should sit under the **umbrella**, you're looking a little toasted.
*PREH-pee na ka-tsees KA-toh ah-POH teen **oh-BREH-la**, EH-hees ka-EE.*
Πρέπει να κάτσεις κάτω από την **ομπρέλα**, έχεις καεί.

····Bathroom
Too-ah-LE-ta
Τουαλέτα

Where's the **bathroom**?
*POO EE-neh ee **too-ah-LEH-ta**?*
Πού είναι η **τουαλέτα**;

Let me take a quick **shower**.
*KA-tse na KA-noh EH-na ghree-gho-ro **dooz**.*
Κάτσε να κάνω ένα γρήγορο **ντουζ**.

The **sink** is clogged.
*VOO-loh-seh oh **neh-roh-HEE-tees**.*
Βούλωσε ο **νεροχύτης**.

Dude, with this color I can go sell CDs in Monastiraki.
Ma-LA-ka, meh TE-tyo HRO-ma bo-ro na poo-LA-oh see-DEE stoh mo-na-stee-RA-kee.
Μαλάκα, με τέτοιο χρώμα μπορώ να πουλάω σιντί στο Μοναστηράκι.
This is a popular way of saying someone has gotten so dark that they could blend in with the boot-legged CD peddlers downtown.

Nice **tan lines** you've got there.
*TEE oh-REH-es **ghra-MEHS** POO-hees KA-nee, ap-toh MAV-reez-ma.*
Τι ωραίες **γραμμές** πού 'χεις κάνει απ' το μαύρισμα.

Wow, **you are so sunburned**! Did you fall asleep in the sun!?
*Poh poh FEE-leh **EH-hees ka-EE pahn-DOO**! Seh PEE-reh oh EE-pnohs MESS-stohn EEL-yoh!?*
Πω πω φίλε **έχεις καεί παντού**! Σε πήρε ο ύπνος μέσ' στον ήλιο;

I'm **peeling** like a snake.
***Xeh-floo-THEE-zoh** sahn FEE-thee.*
Ξεφλουδίζω σαν φίδι.

I haven't **flossed** in months.
*EH-hoh MEE-nes na **KA-noh NEE-ma**.*
Έχω μήνες να **κάνω νήμα**.
You really should. It actually works.

Hey, why don't you get your **dirty laundry** out of the bathroom.
*Na soo poh, yia MA-ze-pse ta **AH-plee-ta** soo AP-toh BA-nyo.*
Να σου πω, για μάζεψε τα **άπλυτα** σου απ' το μπάνιο.

I'm going to go have sex by myself.
PA-oh na KA-noh sex MO-nos moo.
Πάω να κάνω σεξ μόνος μου.
My uncle would say this every time he would go to the bathroom, and it always made me laugh hysterically.

Grab me some **toilet paper.**
*Yia FE-reh moo LEE-gho **ko-LO-har-toh.***
Για φέρε μου λίγο **κωλόχαρτο**.

Literally, "ass paper." Toilet paper is χαρτί υγείας (har-TEE ee-YEE-as).

····Shit, piss, and other stuff

Ska-TA, KA-too-ra, ke lee-PA
Σκατά, κάτουρα και λοιπά

Dude **I need to go take a shit.**
*Ma-LA-ka **HEH-zoo-meh.***
Μαλάκα **χέζομαι**.

I got **the trots.**
*MEH-hee PIA-see **KOH-psee-moh.***
Μ' έχει πιάσει **κόψιμο**.

I need to go take an **emergency shit.**
*PREH-pee na –REE-xoh **EH-na eh-PEE-ghon HEH-see-moh.***
Πρέπει να ρίξω ένα **επειγον χέσιμο**.

I'm going to drop a **deuce.**
*PA-oh yia **hon-DROH.***
Πάω για **χοντρό**.

Those gyros gave me **the runs.**
*MEH PYA-seh **TSEER-la** AP-ta soov-LA-kya.*
Μ' έπιασε **τσίρλα** απ' τα σουβλάκια.

I'm going to go **take a piss.**
*PA-oh na REE-xoh EH-na **ka-TOO-ree-ma.***
Πάω να ρίξω ένα **κατούρημα**.

I'm going to **piss myself.**
*Tha **ka-too-ree-THOH.***
Θα **κατουρηθώ**.

I need to go **pee-pee.**
*THEH-loh na KA-noh **TSEE-sa moo.***
Θέλω να κάνω **τσίσα μου**.

Who farted?
Pee-OS EH-kla-seh?
Ποιος **έκλασε**;

I'm very gassy today.
EH-ho poh-LA ah-EH-ree-ah SEE-meh-ra.
Έχω πολλά **αέρια** σήμερα.

That dude ripped ass, and the whole room cleared out.
EH-ree-xeh MEE-ah kla-NYA oh POO-stees keh AH-thya-seh toh doh-MA-tee-oh.
Έριξε μία κλανιά ο πούστης και άδειασε το δωμάτιο.

I need to blow my nose.
PREH pee na fee-SEE-xoh tee MEE-tee moo.
Πρέπει να **φυσήξω τη μύτη μου**.

Take a look at this big-ass booger.
Ya KEE-ta MEE-ah meex-AH-ra.
Για κοίτα μία **μυξάρα**.

····Under the weather
AH-ro-stos
Άρρωστος

I don't feel good, I'm going home.
PA-oh SPEE-tee, then es-THA-noo-meh ka-LA.
Πάω σπίτι, **δεν αισθάνομαι καλά**.

I feel awful.
Es-THA-noo-meh HAHL-ya.
Αισθάνομαι χάλια.

I'm sick.
EE-meh AH-roh-stohs.
Είμαι άρρωστος.

Dude, I feel like shit.
Ma-LA-ka, es-THA-noo-meh - ska-TA.
Μαλάκα, **αισθάνομαι - σκατά**.

Bring me the thermometer, I think I have a fever.
*FE-reh moo toh **ther-MO-meh-tro**, noh-MEE-zoh pohs*
*EH-hoh **pee-reh-TO**.*
Φέρε μου το **θερμόμετρο**, νομίζω πως έχω **πυρετό**.

I need some…
Hree-AH-zoo-meh…
Χρειάζομαι…

> **pills.**
> *HAHP-ya.*
> χάπια.

> **Medicine.**
> *FAHR-ma-ka.*
> Φάρμακα.

> **aspirin.**
> *ahs-pee-REE-nee.*
> ασπιρίνη.

> **Tylenol.**
> *TAEE-leh-nohl.*
> Τάιλενολ.

> **Advil.**
> *Ahd-VEEL.*
> Αντβίλ.

> **Valium.**
> *VAH-lee-oom.*
> Βάλιουμ.

> **Adirol.**
> *Ah-deh-ROHL.*
> Αντερόλ.

My stomach hurts.
Meh po-NA-ee toh sto-MA-hee moo.
Με πονάει το στομάχι μου.

I have really bad cramps.
*Eh-hoh AHS-hee-mess **KRAH-bess**.*
Έχω άσχημες **κράμπες**.

I'm on the rag.
Eh-hoh peh-REE-oh-thoh.
Έχω περίοδο.
There's really no slang for Aunt Flo in Greek, believe it or not.

I just got my period.
MOH-lees ah-thya-THEH-tee-sa.
Μόλις αδιαθέτησα.

Careful man, she's PMSing.
Ma-LA-ka, PROH-seh-heh, EH-hee LEE-gho pee-em-ES.
Μαλάκα, πρόσεχε, έχει λίγο **PMS**.

I'm going to lie down until my headache goes away.
Tha xa-PLOH-soh MEH-hree na moo FEE-yee oh poh-noh-KEH-fa-los.
Θα ξαπλώσω μέχρι να μου φύγει ο **πονοκέφαλος**.

I'm so nauseous.
MEH-hee PYA-see nahf-TEE-ah.
Μ' έχει πιάσει ναυτία.

I've got really bad heartburn.
Eh-hoh kah-OO-ress.
Έχω **καούρες**.

Don't throw up, or I'll puke too.
Meen kseh-RA-sees, yia-TEE tha KA-noh eh-meh-TOH ke-yho.
Μην **ξεράσεις**, γιατί θα κάνω **εμετό** κι εγώ

I slept funny and now I'm sore everywhere.
Kee-MEE-thee ka stra-VA ke TOH-ra EE-meh pyaz-MEH-nos pa-DOO.
Κοιμήθηκα στραβά και τώρα είμαι **πιασμένος** παντού.

I fell off my bike and twisted my ankle.
EH-pe-se ah-PO toh po-THEE-la-toh ke stra-BOO-lee-ksa tohn ah-STRA-gha-LOH moo.
Έπεσα από το ποδήλατο και **στραμπούλιξα τον αστράγαλό μου**.

I'm **pregnant**!
*EE-meh **EH-gee-ohs**!*
Είμαι **έγκυος**!

Dude, your girlfriend looks **preggers**.
*Ma-LA-ka, ee GOH-meh-NA soo FEH-neh-the LEE-gho **gahs-troh-MEH-nee**.*
Μαλάκα, η γκόμενά σου φαίνεται λίγο **γκαστρωμένη**.

I'm pretty sure **I knocked her up**.
*STA-dahr teen **koo-TOO-poh-sa**.*
Στάνταρ την **κουτούπωσα**.

CHAPTER 5

HORNY GREEK
PROH-STY-HAH EH-LEE-NEE-KA
Πρόστυχα Ελληνικά

So one night Dionysus got Aphrodite fucked up on fermented fig juice and the poor dear woke up with a ripped toga and a marble dildo up her ass. Hey, these things happen from time to time, especially when the local environment is conducive to debauchery. Greece is a very sexy place, and the mere act of spending some time there will definitely coax your inner nympho to come out and play. Ancient dongs aside, you can get yourself laid any way you want; the people are just down to fuck. So much so that it makes us Americans look like missionary-only prudes. Most of Europe makes us look a little boring, but the Greeks that much more so. Pack your Trojans if you're brand loyal—they mainly rock Durex over there—and go get your freak on!

I want to…
THEH-loh na…
Θέλω να...

> **have sex.**
> *KA-noh sehx.*
> κάνω σεξ.

> **make love to you.**
> *soo KA-noh EH-roh-ta*
> σου κάνω έρωτα.
> For when you want to be a little classy.

> **fuck.**
> *gha-MEE-soh.*
> γαμήσω.

> **screw you.**
> *seh Pee-THEE-ksoh.*
> σε πηδήξω.

> **fuck your brains out.**
> *soo peh-TA-ksoh ta MA-tia E-ksoh.*
> σου πετάξω τα μάτια έξω.

> **hit that.**
> *tees tohn foh-REH-soh.*
> της τον φορέσω.

> **give her the D!**
> *tees REE-ksoh EH-na POO-tsoh.*
> της ρίξω έναν πούτσο!

I tore my girlfriend up last night! No fights for a month!
KSEH-skee-sa teen koh-PEH-la moo stohn POO-tsoh hthes toh VRA-thee! Dehn E-hee GRI-nia yia ka-NA MEE-na!
Ξέσκισα την κοπέλα μου στον πούτσο χθες το βράδυ! Δεν έχει γκρίνια για κανά μήνα!
Haha, if only…

Goddamn dude, I was balls deep in that bitch last night!

Poh, malaka moo, teen kseh-PA-toh-sa teen GOH-meh-na hthes toh VRAthee!

Πω, μαλάκα μου, την ξεπάτωσα την γκόμενα χτες το βράδυ!

You can use this phrase with your friends the next morning at the café if you really gave it good and deep to your girl the night before...

A girl like that will give it up for sure.

STA-dar tha soo KA-tsee TEH-tya GOH-meh-na.

Στάνταρ θα σου κάτσει τέτοια γκόμενα.

C'mon let's go for a quickie, it'll just take a minute!

EH-la gia E-na sta GHREE-ghoh-ra, EH-na lep-TOH tha mas PA-ree!

Έλα για ένα στα γρήγορα, ένα λεπτό θα μας πάρει!

I fucked the shit out of that little slut.

Teen kse-KOH-lya-sa teen poo-TA-na.

Την ξεκώλιασα την πουτάνα.

Tonight, I'm making her a woman.

Ah-POH-pseh, thah teen KA-noh yee-NEH-ka.

Απόψε θα την κάνω γυναίκα.

Just relax. Keep in mind that you're probably not going to impress anybody and everything should be okay.

We played just-the-tip with each other.

Tees ton ah-KOO-bee-sa lee-GA-kee.

Της τον ακούμπησα λιγάκι.

This phrase always gets a laugh.

Girl, he really gave it to me last night.

Moh-REE, moo tohn EH-thoh-se ah-GHREE-ohs hthes toh VRA-thee.

Μωρή, μου τον έδωσε αγρίως χτες το βράδυ.

I'm going to analyze her dreams for her, if she keeps on dancing and looking at me like that.

Tha tees ksee-YEE-soh toh OH-nee-roh, AH-ma see-neh-HEE-see na hoh-REH-vee ke na meh koh-ZA-ree EH-tsee.

Θα της 'ξηγήσω το όνειρο, άμα συνεχίσει να χορεύει και να με κοζάρει έτσι.

This is a bit old-fashioned and not used as often anymore. It comes from a time when explicit sexual terminology was a bit more taboo, but it can be very funny when used correctly.

We fucked without a condom.

*Teen GA-mee-sa ho-REES **ka-PO-ta**.*

Τη γάμησα χωρίς **καπότα**.

The normal word for "condom" is προφυλακτικό (*proh-fee-lak-tee-KO*). Seems like you should know this one *too*.

····The shaft

O POO-lohs

Ο πούλος

What can I say, we guys love naming our junk no matter where we're from. Here are some of the most commonly used words to refer to your shlong.

Hey ladies, get a load of my...

Eh, koh-REE-tsya, yia PAHR-teh ghra-MEE toh...

Εεε, κορίτσια, για πάρτε γραμμή το...

> **penis.**
> *PEH-ohs.*
> πέος.
>
> **dick.**
> *poo-LEE.*
> πουλί.
> Literally, "bird," but it's also the most popular way of referring to one's...ego.
>
> **cock.**
> *kahv-LEE.*
> καυλί.

VIRGINITY)))
PAR-THEH-NYA
ΠΑΡΘΕΝΙΑ

There's a first time for everything. . .

Calm down, sailor, I'm still a virgin. (female)
*Ya ee-REH-mee-seh LEE-gho, reh FI-leh,EE-meh ah-KOH-ma **par-THEH-na**.*
Για ηρέμησε λίγο, ρε φίλε, είμαι ακόμα **παρθένα**.

I can't believe you're still a fucking virgin! (male)
*Thehn boh-ROH na pee-STE-psoh pos EE-seh ah-KO-ma **mee-kso-par-THEH-na**!*
Δεν μπορώ να πιστέψω πως είσαι ακόμα **μυξοπαρθένα**!

I'd really like to pop her cherry.
THAHtheh-la poh-LEE na teen kse-pah-rtheh-NYA-soh.
Θα 'θελα πολύ να την ξεπαρθενιάσω.

You really don't. They get super clingy.

I have her virginity in my back pocket.
*EH-ho teen **par-theh-NYA** tees steen TSEH-pee moo.*
Έχω την **παρθενιά** της στην τσέπη μου.

Some dude in a village just outside of Sparta mumbled this saying to me as he shook his whiskey glass toward a girl I later found out be the mayor's daughter. It's stuck with me ever since.

I don't deal with dumbass virgins.
*Then ah-sho-LOO-meh meh **ska-to-par-THEH-nes**.*
Δεν ασχολούμαι με **σκατοπαρθένες**.

I'm a virgin. . .my sign that is.
EE-meh par-THEH-nos sto ZOH-thee-oh.
Είμαι παρθένος...στο ζώδιο.

In English it's Virgo. In Greek it's Virgin. This phrase is a nice way to break the sexual ice without being too forceful.

shlong.
psoh-LEE.
ψωλή.

pee-pee.
tsoo-TSOO-nee.
τσουτσούνι.

Just in case you feel like being childish about the situation.

johnson.
POO-tsohs.
πούτσος.

My god, look at that huge **shlong** that dude has!
*THEHE moo, KEE-ta MEE-ah **psoh-LA-ra** poo EH-hee oh tee-PAHS!*
Θεέ μου, κοίτα μία **ψωλάρα** που έχει ο τυπάς!

I need to find a job. I'm so bored of playing with my **dong** all day.
*PREH-pee na vroh thool-YA. EH-hoh va-reh-THEE na PEH-zoh meh tee **Ma-la-PEHR-tha** moo OH-lee MEH-ra.*
Πρέπει να βρω δουλειά. Έχω βαρεθεί να παίζω με τη **μαλαπέρδα** μου όλη μέρα.

Who wants some **village sausage**?
*Pyohs THEH-lee LEE-ghoh **hor-YA-tee-koh loo-KA-nee-koh**?*
Ποιος θέλει λίγο **χωριάτικο λουκάνικο**;

And here's the **salami**!
*NA-toh to **pah-lah-MAH-ree**!*
Να το **παλαμάρι**!

One of my personal favorites.

DiRTY BOYS)))
PROH-STEE-HAH AH-GOH-RYAH
ΠΡΟΣΤΥΧΑ ΑΓΟΡΙΑ

The next two phrases are funny little sayings that are popular among the local youth.

My cock is a gentleman. It gets up so you can sit down.
Oh POO-tsohs moo EE-neh TZEN-tle-man, see-KOH-neh-teh yia na KA-tsees.
Ο πούτσος μου είναι τζέντλεμαν, σηκώνεται για να κάτσεις.
By "sit down," we mean "sit on it."

My dick is a Green Beret, always standing at attention!
Tsol-YAS oh POO-tsos moo tsol-YAS!
Τσολιάς ο πούτσος μου, τσολιάς!

••••Balls
BA-les
Μπάλες

Just like you kept telling your ex, don't forget the nuts!

Balls
Ar-HEE-thya
Αρχίδια
This word actually comes from the word "orchid." The ancients seemed to think those flowers looked like nuts.

Nuts
Kar-EE-thya
Καρύδια

Two more drinks and I'm giving her the salty nuts.
AH-la thyo poh-TA ke tha tees ksee-yee-THOH al-mee-roh fee-STEE-kee.
Αλλα δυο ποτά και θα της 'ξηγηθώ **αλμυρό φιστίκι**.

This is an old-school phrase that you don't hear very often, but it's hilarious when used correctly. Save it for when you want to be a little goofier than usual.

Come on, baby, play with my nads a little bit.
EH-la, moh-ROH moo, PEH-kse LEE-gho meh ta pa-PAR-ya moo.
Έλα, μωρό μου, παίξε λίγο με τα **παπάρια** μου.

My ex's dog bit me right in the family legacy one time.
Oh SKEE-lohs tees PROH-een moo meh THA-ghoseh steenh ee-koh-GEH-nee-AH moo MEE-ah foh-RA.
Ο σκύλος της πρώην μου με δάγκωσε στην **οικογένειά** μου μία φορά.

····Boobs
Vee-ZYA
Βυζιά

The most common way to refer to a lady's ladies is βυζιά (vee-ZYA), and the following terms are all variations on this word. Know these well and you'll be covered, since the rest are noticibly less popular.

She's got perky tits now, but wait 'til she gets a few years on her.
EH-hee KAH-tee sfeeh-TA vee-ZOH-ba-la TOH-ra, ah-LA KA-tse na PAH-ree meh-ree-KA hroh-NAH-kya.
Έχει κάτι σφιχτά **βυζόμπαλα** τώρα, αλλά κάτσε να πάρει μερικά χρονάκια.

My god, look at those big-ass titties! Her fucking bra can't contain them!
THEHE moo KEE-ta KAH-tee vee-ZA-ress! Then ta kra-TA-ee toh soo-TYEN tees!
Θέε μου, κοίτα κάτι **βυζάρες**! Δεν τα κρατάει το **σουτιέν** της!

Squeeze my...
ZOO-lee-KSE moo ...
Ζούληξέ μου...

Can I play with your...?
Boh-ROH na PEH-kso me...?
Μπορώ να παίξω με..;

> **breasts.**
> *sTEE-thos.*
> στήθος.

> **melons.**
> *pe-PO-nya.*
> πεπόνια.

> **rack.**
> *bal-KOH-nya.*
> μπαλκόνια.

Get your jugs out of the way, lady!
MA-zeh-pseh tah Mas-TA-rya soo, kee-RA moo!
Μάζεψε τα **μαστάρια** σου, κυρά μου!
This one is a little crude, so tread lightly.

Hey, are your nipples pierced?
EH-hees KAH-nee PEER-seeng stees ROH-yes soo?
Έχεις κάνει πίρσινγκ στις **ρώγες** σου;

Just as long as they're perky...
Ar-KEE na EE-neh stee-TA...
Αρκεί να είναι **στητά**...

····Vagina
KOLL-pohs
Κόλπος

There really is a shortage of names for the clam in Greek. It's weird considering how many different ways there are to refer to the male equivalent. Μουνί is used pretty much exclusively, so as long as you know that one, you're basically good.

You know what you need? Some pussy.
*KSE-rees tee hree-AH-zeh-seh? LEE-gho **moo-NEE**.*
Ξέρεις τι χρειάζεσαι; Λίγο **μουνί**.

Let me eat your box baby.
*AH-seh meh na YLEE-psoh toh **moo-NA-kee** soo moh-ROH moo.*
Άσε με να γλείψω το **μουνάκι** σου, μωρό μου.

I'm telling you dude, play with her pussy lips next time.
*Soo LEH-oh, re ma-LA-ka, PEH-kse meh ta **moo-NOH-hee-la** tees teen eh-POH-meh-nee FOH-ra.*
Σου λέω, ρε μαλάκα, παίξε με τα **μουνόχειλά** της την επόμενη φορά.

I just couldn't dude, her thing smelled like fish.
*Then boh-ROO-sa, reh, VROH-ma-yeh toh **PRAH-ma** tees psa-REE-la.*
Δεν μπορούσα, ρε, βρόμαγε το **πράμα** της ψαρίλα.

Don't be so pussy whipped bro!
*Meen EE-seh TOH-soh **moo-NOH-thoo-lohs**, reh ah-THER-feh!*
Μην είσαι τόσο **μουνόδουλος**, ρε αδερφέ!

····Butt
KO-loss
Κώλος

I'm not an ass man per se, but you have to tip your hat whenever you see a good one.

Booty
Po-POHS
Ποπός

Rear
Pee-see-NOHS
Πισινός

Hindquarters
Oh-PEE-sthee-ah
Οπίσθια

Look at that ass!
*KEE-ta EH-na **koh-LEE**!*
Κοίτα ένα **κωλί**!

Seriously though, I don't like a huge ass.
*Hoh-REES PLA-ka, OH-mohs, then poh-LEE ghoo-STA-roh AH-ma EH-hee **ko-LA-ra**.*
Χωρίς πλάκα, όμως, δεν πολυ-γουστάρω άμα έχει **κωλάρα**.

I'm going to bite you right on the butt cheek.
*Thah seh thaGOH-soh stoh **ko-lo-MA-ghoo-lo**.*
Θα σε δαγκώσω στο **κωλομάγουλο**.

We were both kinda drunk, so I put it right in her booty hole just like that.
*EE-ma-stahn ke ee THEE-oh psee-lo-meh-theez-MEH-nee, ke tees tohn EH-va-la steen **ko-lo-tree-PEE-tha**, EH-tsee ah-PLOS.*
Ήμασταν και οι δύο ψιλομεθυσμένοι και της τον έβαλα στην **κωλοτρυπίδα**, έτσι απλώς.

····Oral sex
Sto-ma-tee-KOS EH-ro-tas
Στοματικός έρωτας

In Greek, you don't say "suck my this" or "suck my that." The typical phrases aren't so direct. Don't get me wrong, they're just as crude, but they beat around the bush just a little bit.

Tell her the **blow job** is an art form and should be studied.
*Pess tees poss toh **tsee-BOO-kee** EE-neh TEHH-nee ke hree-AH-zeh-teh meh-LEH-tee.*
Πες της πως το **τσιμπούκι** είναι τέχνη και χρειάζεται μελέτη.

Suck my dick.
PA-reh moo mya PEE-pa.
Πάρε μου μια πίπα.
Loosely translates to "give me pipe."

She **blew me** the entire drive home.
*Moo **PEE-reh tsee-BOO-kee** OH-lo toh THRO-mo MEH-hree toh SPEE-tee.*
Μου **πήρε τσιμπούκι** όλο το δρόμο μέχρι το σπίτι.

I've heard she **plays the clarinet**.
*EH-hoh ah-KOO-see poss **PEH-zee SOH-loh kla-REE-noh**.*
Έχω ακούσει πως **παίζει σόλο κλαρίνο**.

That girl's a real **dick sucker**.
*EE-neh po-LEE **tsee-book-LOO** ee GO-meh-na.*
Είναι πολύ **τσιμπουκλού** η γκόμενα.

Suck on my pipe so I can quit smoking.
***PA-reh moo mya PEE-pa** yia na KO-pso toh tsee-GA-ro.*
Πάρε μου μια πίπα για να κόψω το τσιγάρο.
This phrase is an old-school play on words, since πίπα literally means a tobacco pipe.

She was **bossing me up** for hours.
Moo ton pee-PEE-lee-zeh yia OH-ress.
Μου τον πιπίλιζε για ώρες.

My boyfriend's great at **eating pussy**.
*Toh ah-GHO-ree moo EE-neh PROH-tohs sta **ylee-fo-MOO-nya**.*
Το αγόρι μου είναι πρώτος στα **γλειφομούνια**.

You're really lucky, you **go down on me** so well.
*EH-heh HA-ree poo EE-seh ka-LOHS sta **ylee-PSEE-ma-ta**.*
Έχε χάρη που είσαι καλός στα **γλειψίματα**.

····What's your favorite position?

Pya EE-neh ee ah-ga-pee-MEH-nee soo STA-see?
Ποια είναι η αγαπημένη σου στάση;

My favorite position is…
Ee STAH-see poo proh-tee-MOH EE-neh…
Η στάση που προτιμώ είναι…

> **missionary.**
> *eeh-eh-rah-poh-stoh-li-KO.*
> ιεραποστολικό.
>
> **doggy-style.**
> *pi-soh-kol-lee-TO.*
> πισωκολλητό.
>
> **girl on top.**
> *ah-log-AH-ki.*
> αλογάκι.
>
> **69.**
> *eh-KSEE-da eh-NEH-ah.*
> εξήντα εννέα.
>
> **anal.**
> *oh-thoh-ma-nee-KO.*
> οθωμανικό.

standing up.
sta OR-thee-ah.
στα όρθια.

side by side.
pla-ya-STOH.
στο πλάι.

titty fucking.
ee-spa-NEE-ko.
ισπανικό.

My girl is so hot, I really want to make a porno with her.
EE-neh TOH-soh moo-NA-ra toh koh-REE-tsee moo, poo THEH-loh PA-ra poh-lee na KA-noh MEE-ah TSO-da ma-ZEE tees.
Είναι τόσο μουνάρα το κορίτσι μου, που θέλω πάρα πολύ να κάνω μία **τσόντα** μαζί της.

You want me to slide a finger in your butt?
THEHlees na soo VA-lo LEE-gho ko-lo-THAH-tee-lo?
Θέλεις να σου βάλω λίγο **κωλοδάχτυλο**;

So where did we land on that threesome?
POS kah-tah-LEE-kash-meh sto tree-oh-LEH?
Πώς καταλήξαμε στο **τριολέ**;

There's going to be an orgy at the hotel.
Tha PEH-ksee OR-yee-oh sto kse-noh-tho-HEE-oh.
Θα παίξει **όργιο** στο ξενοδοχείο.

I fingered her right in the middle of the club.
Tees EH-va-la THA-htee-lo mes-sto klab.
Της έβαλα δάχτυλο μέσα στο κλαμπ.

ORGASM)))
OR-GHAZ-MOHS
ΟΡΓΑΣΜΟΣ

I'm coming!
HEE-no!
Χύνω!

Oh god, I'm gonna come!
Oh, theh-EH moo, thah HEE-soh!
Ωχ, θέε μου, θα χύσω!

Here comes the jizz...
*OH-pa, EHR-hon-de ta **FLOH-kya**...*
Ώπα, έρχονται τα **φλόκια**...

Don't stop, don't stop!
Mee stah-mah-TAS, mee stah-mah-TAS!
Μη σταματάς, μη σταματάς!

I came all over her face!
Teen EH-hee-sa stee MA-pa!
Την έχυσα στη μάπα!

Dude, she swallowed all of it!
Ma-LA-ka, ta ka-TA-pye OH-la!
Μαλάκα, τα κατάπιε όλα!

Let's try for **multiple orgasms.**
*PA-meh yia **po-la-PLOOS or-gaz-MOOS**.*
Πάμε για **πολλαπλούς οργασμούς**.

••••Weird shit
Per-EE-er-ga PRAH-gmah-ta
Περίεργα πράγματα

The ancients used to get into all kinds of kinky shit, so why wouldn't their descendants? Hey man, to each their own. Nobody's judging here.

Are you into any sort of fetish?
*EH-hees KA-na **VEE-tsyoh**?*
Έχεις κάνα **βίτσιο**;

My girl is really kinky.
*EE-neh po-LEE **vee-TSYO-za** ee ko-PEH-la moo.*
Είναι πολύ **βιτσιόζα** η κοπέλα μου.

That dirty old man just grabbed my ass!
*MOH-lees meh HOOF-toh-seh oh **por-NOH-yer-os**!*
Μόλις με χούφτωσε ο **πορνόγερος**!

Did you really just try to dick slap me!?
*Soh-va-RA PEE-yes na moo REE-ksees **poo-tso-SKA-bee-lo**?*
Σοβαρά πήγες να μου ρίξεις **πουτσοσκάμπιλο**;

She told me to choke her a little bit.
*MOO-peh na teen **PNEE-kso** LEE-gho.*
Μου 'πε να την **πνίξω** λίγο.

It's obvious that priest is a pedo.
*FEH-neh-the pos EE-neh **peh-THE-ras** oh pa-PAS.*
Φαίνεται πως είναι **παιδέρας** ο παπάς.
I'm just saying, there's a bit of a trend.

I'm for sure a nympho.
*STA-dar EE-meh **NEEM-pho-MA-nees**.*
Στάνταρ είσαι **νυμφομανής**.

You wanna try a little S&M?
*Thehs na tho-kee-MA-soo-meh LEE-gho **ES-en-em**?*
Θες να δοκιμάσουμε λίγο **Σ&Μ**;

Can I tie you up?
Boh-ROH na seh THEH-so?
Μπορώ να σε δέσω;

····Solo action and sexual problems
Ma-la-KEE-es keh seh-ksoo-ah-lee-KA proh-VLEE-ma-ta
Μαλακίες και σεξουαλικά προβλήματα

Sometimes, if you want something done right, or at all, you've got to do it yourself. You're not going to get lucky every night, so here are a few ways to tell your friends that you ended up slapping the ham.

I'm going to go have sex by myself.
*PA-oh na **KA-noh** sex **MO-nos** moo.*
Πάω να **κάνω σεξ μόνος** μου.

I'm jerking off and going to sleep.
*Tha **teen PEH-kso** ke tha teen PEH-so.*
Θα **την παίξω** και θα την πέσω.
This is supposed to rhyme.

I'm going home to play with my vibrator.
*PA-oh SPEE-tee na PE-ksoh meh tohn **thoh-nee-TEE** moo.*
Πάω σπίτι να παίξω με το **δονητή** μου.

Dude, I couldn't get it up for shit.
*Ma-LA-ka, **then moo see-ko-noh-ta-neh** meh TEE-po-ta.*
Μαλάκα, **δεν μου σηκωνόταν** με τίποτα.

Fuck it, let's go get a couple of whores.
*GHA-ma toh, PA-meh yia **poo-TA-nes**.*
Γάμα το, πάμε για **πουτάνες**.

····Homosexuality
Oh-mo-fee-lo-fee-LEE-ah
Ομοφυλοφιλία

Ain't nothin' wrong with dude-on-dude in Greece. They've been okay with it since ancient times. Sure, there are assholes who'll make a joke or two at your expense, but no one's going to lynch you if you like the penis. And, of course, I have yet to meet a guy who has a problem with girl-on-girl.

Homosexual
Oh-mo-fee-LO-fee-los
Ομοφυλόφιλος

Gay
Geh-EE
Γκέι

Queer
Ah-NO-ma-los
Ανώμαλος

Homo
POOS-tees
Πούστης

Fag
POO-stra
Πούστρα

The Greek for "homo" and "fag" can be used pretty much interchangeably. The latter tends to be a little harsher, but in general, they aren't considered to be as derogatory as their English counterparts.

That kid's a little fruity.
*EE-neh LEE-go **poos-TEH-rle** to peh-THEE.*
Είναι λίγο **πουστερλέ** το παιδί.

For sure he takes it up the ass.
STA-dahr tohn PEHR-nee.
Στάνταρ τον παίρνει.

That old queer always complains about the music.
OH-lo gree-NYA-zee yia tee moo-see-KEE ee Yeh-ro-POO-stra.
Όλο γκρινιάζει για τη μουσική η **γεροπούστρα**.

Lesbian
Lez-VEE-ah
Λεσβία

Dyke
Dzee-VEE-dzee-loo
Ντζιβιντζιλού

She's butch like a truck driver.
EE-neh sahn da-lee-KEH-rees.
Είναι σαν **νταλικέρης**.

Transvestite
Tra-veh-STEE
Τραβεστί

Tranny
Tra-VEH-lee
Τραβέλι

••••STDs and Abortions
SEE-NEE-MEE keh ek-TROH-sees
ΣΝΜ και εκτρώσεις

Sometimes, the lovin's so good that you need to pay for it in order to restore balance to the universe. Nothing is free in this world. Here's hoping that no one has to pay the following prices, but just in case, this is the vocab you need to know.

Stay away, dude, that bitch is really dirty.
Ma-kree-AH, ma-LA-ka, EE-neh po-LEE VRO-mee-kee af-TEE ee GO-meh-na.
Μακριά, μαλάκα, είναι πολύ **βρόμικη** αυτή η γκόμενα.

She didn't tell me she had herpes.
Then moo EE-peh OH-tee EH-hee Er-PEE.
Δεν μου είπε ότι έχει **έρπή**.

The beggar on the subway was saying he had **AIDS**.
O zee-TYA-nos sto meh-TRO EH-le-yeh OH-tee EH-hee
EH-ee-dz.
Ο ζητιάνος στο μετρό έλεγε πως έχει **AIDS**.
This is a common occurrence on the Athens subway.

I could smell the **gonorrhea** from the hallway.
*Vro-ma-yeh **vle-VO-ree-ah** AP-toh THYA-thro-moh.*
Βρόμαγε **βλεννόρροια** απ' το διάδρομο.

Holy fuck, I'm **pregnant**!
*Gha-moh toh hree-STOH mooEE-meh **EH-gee-os**!*
Γαμώ τον Χριστό μου, είμαι **έγκυος**!

She's **knocked up** to her ears.
*EE-neh **Ga-stro-MEH-nee** MEH-hree ta af-TYA.*
Είναι **γκαστρωμένη** μέχρι τα αφτιά.

I have to get an **abortion**.
*PREH-pee na KA-noh **EH-ktro-see**.*
Πρέπει να κάνω **έκτρωση**.

Can you pick me up a **pregnancy test**?
*Boh-REES na moo FEH-rees EH-na **test eh-gee-moh-SEE-nees**?*
Μπορείς να μου φέρεις ένα **τεστ εγκυμοσύνης**;

CHAPTER 6

ANGRY GREEK
TSAN-DEES-MEH-NA EH-LEE-NEE-KA
Τσαντισμένα Ελληνικά

Let's face it, this is the first chapter you're going to read. Few things are as important as being able to tell the bouncer or the asshole cab driver to go fuck himself, no matter where in the world you might be. One must always be prepared. So go ahead and arm yourself with as many linguistic weapons as you can; there are definitely plenty to choose from. Most Greeks tend to bark more than they bite, but the right combination of selections from this chapter is sure to make anybody take a swing. Proceed with caution.

····You gotta problem?

EH-hees PROH-vlee-ma?
Έχεις πρόβλημα;

The beginning of every good fight involves a little communication to establish the presence of an issue. You know, something along the lines of "What the fuck is your problem?"

What's wrong with you?
Tee EH-hees?
Τι έχεις;

Is something up?
PEH-zee KA-tee?
Παίζει κάτι;

Can I help you with something?
Thes KA-tee?
Θες κάτι;
As you can imagine, this is meant to be said with a hint of sarcasm.

What do you want, dude?
Tee thes, reh FEE-leh?
Τι θες, ρε φίλε;

Do you have a problem, because you've been looking at me weird all night.
EH-hees PRO-vlee-ma, yia-TEE meh koh-ZA-rees OH-lee NEEH-ta.
Έχεις πρόβλημα, γιατί **με κοζάρεις** όλη νύχτα.

You look a little off. Is something going on?
FEH-neh-seh LEE-go peh-REE-er-ghos. TREH-hee KA-tee?
Φαίνεσαι λίγο περίεργος. **Τρέχει κάτι**;

Is something wrong with her?
TREH-hee TEE-poh-ta ma-FTEE?
Τρέχει τίποτα μ' αυτή;

What's your fucking problem?
Tee ZO-ree tra-VAS?
Τι ζόρι τραβάς;

Are you looking for trouble?
PSA-hneh-seh giah kah-VGAH?
Ψάχνεσαι για καβγά;

Did you say something tough guy?
EE-pes KA-tee, reh MA-nga?
Είπες κάτι, ρε **μάγκα**;

What the fuck do you want from me!?
Tee thes AP-tee zoh-EE moo!?
Τι θες απ' τη ζωή μου;

This is a good one to use when you just can't take someone anymore and all you want them to do is spontaneously combust so they'll leave you the fuck alone.

····You're pissing me off
Meh tsan-DEE-zees
Με τσαντίζεις

Good etiquette states that you do a little barking before you start biting. It seems only fair to give the asshole on the other side of the argument a bit of a warning.

Don't piss me off.
Mee moo tee-SPAS.
Μη μου τη σπας.

Go to hell!
AH-ee stohn DYA-voh-loh!
Άι στον διάβολο!

You're really starting to get on my nerves.
EH-hees ar-HEE-see na moo SPAS tah NEV-ra.
Έχεις αρχίσει να μου σπας τα νεύρα.

I'm about to lose it any minute, dude.
Thah treh-LA-thoh OH-poo NA-neh, ma-LA-ka.
Θα τρελαθώ όπου να' ναι, μαλάκα.

I really cursed that asshole out.
Tohn EH-vree-sa poh-LEE AHS-hee-ma tohn ma-LA-ka.
Τον έβρισα πολύ άσχημα τον μαλάκα.

This chick is annoying the hell out of me.
Moo PREE-zee ta pa-PAR-ya ee GOH-meh-na.
Μου πρήζει τα παπάρια η γκόμενα.

I think there's been a misunderstanding.
*Noh-MEE-zoh pos EH-yee-neh **par-eh-KSEE-yee-see**.*
Νομίζω πως έγινε **παρεξήγηση**.

Please don't get me riled up tonight.
Mee meh tsee-TOH-nees ah-PO-pseh seh pa-ra-ka-LO.
Μη με τσιτώνεις απόψε σε παρακαλώ.

Leave me alone, I'm sick and tired off you.
*AH-seh meh, SEH-hoh **skee-loh-vah-reh-THEE**.*
Άσε με, σ' έχω **σκυλοβαρεθεί**.

Look, his blood is boiling.
*KEE-ta, VRA-zee toh **EH-ma too**.*
Κοίτα, βράζει το **αίμα του**.
This phrase can also be used to describe someone who is just young and full of energy and emotion as well as someone who is pissed the fuck off.

Why do you insist on pushing all of my fucking buttons?
*Ya-TEE eh-pee-MEH-nees na moo pa-TAS OH-la ta **yha-mee-MEH-na** moo koo-BIA?*
Γιατί επιμένεις να μου πατάς όλα τα **γαμημένα** μου κουμπιά;

I got really angry and I yelled at him.
*Tsan-DEE-stee-ka PA-ra poh-LEE ke too **EH-va-la tees fo-NESS**.*
Τσαντίστηκα πάρα πολύ και του **έβαλα τις φωνές**.

I snapped.
EH-yhee-na TOOR-kos.
Έγινα Τούρκος.
Literally, "I became a Turk." This popular phrase gives you a bit of a taste of the lingering animosity between the Greeks and the Turks.

····Fighting
XEE-lo
Ξύλο

I'm gonna...
Thah seh...
Θα σε...

> **hit you.**
> *va-REH-soh.*
> βαρέσω.

> **kick your ass.**
> *pla-KOH-soh stoh XEE-loh.*
> πλακώσω στο ξύλο.

> **hurt you.**
> *THEE-ro.*
> δείρω.

> **tan your hide.**
> *tsa-KEE-soh.*
> τσακίσω.

You ain't gonna do shit!
Tha moo KLA-sees t-ar-HEE-theea!
Θα μου κλάσεις τ' αρχίδια!

We got into a fist fight.
Pla-koh-THEE-ka-meh stoh KSEE-loh.
Πλακωθήκαμε στο ξύλο.

I fucked him up.
Too EH-spa-sa ta MOO-tra.
Του έσπασα τα μούτρα.

We really got into a serious scrap.
YEE-na-meh KOH-los.
Γίναμε κώλος.
This phrase is best used when the scene gets really ugly.

····WTF!?

Tee ston POO-tso!?
Τι στον Πούτσο;

Are you serious!?
Soh-va-ro-lo-YEES!?
Σοβαρολογείς;

I can't stand that bitch.
Then teen an-DE-ho tee ma-LA-ko.
Δεν την αντέχω τη μαλάκω.

What the hell just happened?
Tee EH-yee-neh MOH-lees TOH-ra?
Τι έγινε μόλις τώρα;

There's no way what you're saying is true.
Then PEH-zee af-TOH poo les.
Δεν παίζει αυτό που λες.

What the hell are you talking about?
Tee les TOH-ra?
Τι λες τώρα;

I just can't **believe** you.
*Then bo-RO na seh **pees-TEH-pso**.*
Δεν μπορώ να σε **πιστέψω**.

Hate
MEE-sos
Μίσος

I **hate** you.
*Seh **mee-SO**.*
Σε **μισώ**.

You're **unbearable**.
*EE-seh **ah-nee-POH-foh-ros**.*
Είσαι **ανυπόφορος**.

····Fuck!
Gha-MO toh!
Γαμώτο!

In Greece the F-bomb isn't as taboo as it is in the U.S. The mere act of yelling "fuck" isn't going to get you into too much trouble. It would be the equivalent of yelling "damn it." It's what you fuck that adds gravity to the situation. "Fuck my luck" is no big deal. "Fuck your mother" on the other hand…them's fightin' words.

Fuck you!
AH-nde gha-MEE-soo!
Άντε γαμήσου!

Fuck it.
GHA-ma toh.
Γάμα το.

Give me/us a fucking break!
GHA-mee-seh mas!
Γάμησέ μας!

I will fuck you up.
Tha seh gha-MEE-so.
Θα σε γαμήσω.

I can't find my fucking keys.
*Then boh-ROH na vroh ta **gha-mee-MEH-na** ta klee-DYA moo.*
Δεν μπορώ να βρω τα **γαμημένα** τα κλειδιά μου.

You've got a cornucopia of things to fuck. Keep this list in mind, and you'll never be at a loss for words. When you say "fuck my" you're showing anger at a situation. When you say "fuck your," you're showing anger to someone. Either can be used with any one of the following.

Fuck…
Gha-MOH…
Γαμώ…

> **my Virgin Mary.**
> *teen Pa-na-YEE-ah moo.*
> την Παναγία μου.
>
> **my Christ.**
> *tohn Hree-STOH moo.*
> τον Χριστό μου.
>
> **your god.**
> *tohn theh-OH soo.*
> τον θεό σου.
>
> **my antichrist.**
> *tohn aah-DEE-hree-STO moo.*
> τον αντίχριστό μου
>
> **your mother.**
> *tee MA-na soo.*
> τη μάνα σου.
>
> **my family.**
> *toh SOH-ee moo.*
> το σόι μου.

LIAR)))
PSE-FTEE
ΨΕΥΤΗ

You're a liar.
EE-seh PSEF-tees.
Είσαι ψεύτης.

Are you **fucking** with me!?
*Meh **thoo-LEV-ees**!?*
Με **δουλεύεις**;

Don't **lie** to me.
*Mee moo **less PSEH-ma-ta**.*
Μη μου λες **ψέματα**.

I don't **believe** you at all.
*Then seh **pees-TE-voh** ka-THOH-loo.*
Δεν σε **πιστεύω** καθόλου.

Don't listen to him, he always talks out of his ass.
Meen tohn ah-KOOS, LEH-ee OH-loh ma-la-KEE-es.
Μην τον ακούς, λέει όλο μαλακίες.

Don't believe him dude. Everything he says is a lie.
*Meen ton pee-STE-vees, re. LEH-ee OH-lo **ma-la-KI-ess**.*
Μην τον πιστεύεις, ρε. Λέει όλο **μαλακίες**.

my kin.
tee FA-ra moo.
τη φάρα μου.

your mother's pussy.
toh moo-NEE tees MA-nas soo.
το μουνί της μάνας σου.

the pussy that spit you out.
toh moo-NEE poo seh PEH-ta-kseh.
το μουνί που σε πέταξε.

This one is really rough, so use it very sparingly.

my team.

teen pa-na-ha-ee-KEE moo.

την Παναχαϊκή μου.

Παναχαϊκή is a Greek soccer team. This phrase is used mainly to be funny while avoiding saying Παναγία (Virgin Mary). You don't need to be at a soccer game to say it.

my faith.

teen PEES-tee moo.

την πίστη μου.

your cross.

toh stav-RO soo.

το σταυρό σου.

your evangelist.

tee va-ge-LEE-stra soo.

τη Βαγγελίστρα σου.

my bad luck.

teen ah-tee-HEE-ah moo.

την ατυχία μου.

my brains.

tah mya-LA moo.

τα μυαλά μου.

my life.

tee zoh-EE moo.

τη ζωή μου.

····Shit talking
THA-psee-moh
Θάψιμο

Whether it's to their face or behind their back, shit talking is a pastime everywhere.

That dude is a...
Oh TEE-pos EE-neh...
Ο τύπος είναι...

fucker.
yham-YOH-lees.
γαμιόλης.

dumbass.
TOOV-lo.
τούβλο.

retard.
ka-theeh-steh-ree-MEH-nohs.
καθυστερημένος.

moron.
ee-LEE-theeh-OS.
ηλίθιος.

douche.
ahr-HEE-thee.
αρχίδι.

That chick is a...
Af-tee ee GHO-meh-na EE-neh...
Αυτή η γκόμενα είναι...

slut.
poo-TA-na.
πουτάνα.

bitch.
SKEE-la.
σκύλα.

skank.
TSOO-la.
τσούλα.

cunt.
PEE-pa.
πίπα.

snatch.
kahr-YOH-la.
καριόλα.

bimbo.
GHLA-stra.
γλάστρα.

Why are you prying into my personal shit?
Yia-TEE HOH-neh-se sta proh-soh-pee-KA moo?
Γιατι χώνεσαι στα προσωπικά μου;

You're so fucking **worthless**.
*EE-seh **yia ton POO-tso**.*
Είσαι **για τον πούτσο**.

Why am I even talking to you, you're fucking **useless**.
*Tee KA-thoh-meh ke soo me-LA-oh, ah-FOO EE-seh **AH-hree-stohs**.*
Τι κάθομαι και σου μιλάω, αφού είσαι **άχρηστος**.

You're not acting right, buddy.
Then EE-seh sos-TOS, reh FEE-le.
Δεν είσαι σωστός, ρε φίλε.

Your mama's looking for you, **pussy**.
*Seh PSA-hnee ee MA-na soo, **FLOH-reh**.*
Σε ψάχνει η μάνα σου, **φλώρε**.

Watch your mouth, you jackass!
*PROH-she-heh pohs mee-LAS, reh **yha-ee-THOO-ree**!*
Πρόσεχε πώς μιλάς, ρε **γαϊδούρι**!

Jesus Christ, you're such an asshole!
*THEH-eh moo, tee **ka-THEE-kee** poo EE-seh!*
Θεέ μου, τι **καθίκι** που είσαι!

You can't be that stupid.
*Then PEH-zee na EE-seh **TOH-soh ma-LA-kas**.*
Δεν παίζει να είσαι **τόσο μαλάκας**.

Dude, you're really out of line.
***Yha-MYEH-seh**, reh FEE-leh.*
Γαμιέσαι, ρε φίλε.

One more word out of you and we're done.
AH-lee MEE-ah LE-ksee ke tha soo KOH-pso teen ka-lee-MEH-ra.
Άλλη μια λέξη και θα σου κόψω την καλημέρα.

She's just fucking him for his money.
Tohn pee-THA-ee yia ta lef-TA too.
Τον πηδάει για τα λεφτά του.

The Italian suit was exactly what you needed, you **redneck**.
*Toh ee-ta-lee-KO kos-TOO-mee soo EH-lee-pe, reh **bas-too-NOH-vla-heh**.*
Το ιταλικό κοστούμι σου έλειπε, ρε **μπαστουνόβλαχε**.

That **mama's boy** thinks he's hot shit.
*Teen EH-hee thee theh-OS oh **BOO-lees**.*
Την έχει δει θεός ο **μπούλης**.

Easy Casanova, we all know you're dating your palm.
See-YHA reh yha-MYA, ah-FOO meh teen pa-LA-mee soo tee VYHA-zees PEH-ra.
Σιγά ρε γαμιά, αφού με την παλάμη σου τη βγάζεις πέρα.

You think you're a badass but you're not.
Teen EH-hees thee KA-pos ke then soo PA-ee.
Την έχεις δει κάπως και δεν σου πάει.

It's funny that you think you're in the right.
Moo ah-REH-see poo PSA-hnees ke toh THEE-kee-oh soo.
Μου αρέσει που ψάχνεις και το δίκιο σου.

····Who cares?
Pyee-OS HES-tee-ke?
Ποιος χέστηκε;

All Greeks are masters of indifference, so there are quite a few ways to let people know that you just don't give a fuck.

I don't care.
Then meh NYA-zee.
Δεν με νοιάζει.

I don't give a shit about you!
HES-tee-ka yia teen PAR-tee soo!
Χέστηκα για την πάρτη σου!

SWEAR WORDS)))
VREE-SEE-DEE-AH
ΒΡΙΣΙΔΙΑ

Shit!
Skah-TAH!
Σκατά!

Damn!
Gah-MOH!
Γαμώ!

Dammit!
Gah-MOH-toh!
Γαμώτο!

Oh, fuck!
GAH-mah-tah!
Γάματα!

Holy crap!
O-hee, reh POO-stee!
Όχι, ρε πούστη!

Jesus Christ!
Hree-STƐ moo!
Χριστέ μου!

Motherfucker!
Gah-mee-OH-lee!
Γαμιόλη!

Goddamn it!
Toh KƐ-rah-TOH moo!
Το κέρατό μου!

I don't care what you're going to do.
Then meh en-thya-FER-ee tee tha KA-nees.
Δεν με ενδιαφέρει τι θα κάνεις.

Your problem not mine, big guy.
PROH-vlee-MA soo, meh-YHA-le.
Πρόβλημά σου, μεγάλε.

I don't give a fuck!
Stohn POO-tso moo!
Στον πούτσο μου!

True story, bro.
Ke EE-ha MEE-ah fa-YHOO-ra.
Και είχα μια φαγούρα.

Different strokes for different folks.
Oh ka-THEH-nas meh teen KAV-la too.
Ο καθένας με την καύλα του.

It doesn't matter anymore.
Then EH-hee see-ma-SEE-ah pya.
Δεν έχει σημασία πια.

It is what it is.
Tee na KA-nees?
Τι να κάνεις;

····Enough!
FTA-nee!
Φτάνει!

Shut up!
SKA-she!
Σκάσε!

Get off my ass!
Pa-RA-ta meh! Παράτα με!

Please leave me alone.
AH-seh meh EE-see-ho seh pa-ra-ka-LO.
Άσε με ήσυχο σε παρακαλώ.

You have to stop dealing with that asshole.
*PREH-pee na sta-ma-TEE-sees na as-hoh-LEE-seh
meh tohn ma-LA-ka.*
Πρέπει να σταματήσεις να **ασχολείσαι** με τον μαλάκα.

Dude, drop it.
Xeh-KOH-la, reh ma-LA-ka.
Ξεκόλλα, ρε μαλάκα.

Shut up before I shut you up.
VOO-los-toh preen stoh voo-LO-so eh-GHO.
Βούλωσ' το πριν στο βουλώσω εγώ.

Quit your bullshit.
*Teh-LEE-oh-neh meh tees **ma-la-KEE-es** soo.*
Τελείωνε με τις **μαλακίες** σου.

Get the fuck out of my face.
Xeh-koo-BEE-soo ah-POH broh-STA moo.
Ξεκουμπίσου από μπροστά μου.
Or you could just say ξεκουμπίσου.

I can't keep fighting about stupid shit.
*Then boh-ROH na **tsa-KOH-noh-meh** AH-loh yia ma-la-KEE-es.*
Δεν μπορώ να **τσακώνομαι** άλλο για μαλακίες.

You killed it.
Toh KOO-ra-ses toh THEH-ma.
Το κούρασες το θέμα.

CHAPTER 7

POPPY GREEK
MOH-THA-TA EH-LEE-NEE-KA
Μοδάτα Ελληνικά

What's a party without music, right? Fortunately for you, the soundtrack is in English. The Greek music scene is filled with just as much beat, slap, bass, rock, and Katy Perry as we have stateside. In fact, they get MTV straight out of the UK, as well as the local version of MAD TV. The world's finest entertainers frequently grace the public's ears with their presence, and their after-parties are legendary. Don't get me wrong, local music is also popular, and extremely well represented. For all the foreign musical presence in the country, there is just as much if not more of the local variety. Long story short, whatever you like to chill, vibe, rock out, or just listen to music, Greece has you covered.

••••Music
Moo-see-KEE
Μουσική

What kind of music do you listen to?
Tee moo-see-KEE ah-KOOS?
Τι **μουσική** ακούς;

I like your musical style.
Ghoo-STA-roh ta moo-see-KA GHOO-sta soo.
Γουστάρω τα **μουσικά γούστα** σου.

I can't stand very loud music.
Thehn ah-DEH-hoh teen poh-LEE thee-na-TEE moo-see-KEE.
Δεν αντέχω την **πολύ δυνατή μουσική**.

This shit is bumpin'!
Va-RA-ee toh gha-mee-MEH-noh!
Βαράει το γαμημένο!

Did you hear the new Paparizou song?
AH-koo-sess toh ke-NOOR-yoh tra-GHOO-thee tees Pa-pa-REE-zoo?
Άκουσες το καινούργιο **τραγούδι** της Παπαρίζου;

Elena Paparizou is the Katy Perry of Greece. She sings mainly in Greek, but she also has a decent number of English songs.

What's your favorite band?
Py-OH EE-neh toh ah-gha-pee-MEH-noh soo see-GROH-tee-ma?
Ποιο είναι το αγαπημένο σου **συγκρότημα**;

Fuck yeah, man, I got tickets for the concert!
EH-tsee, reh ma-LA-ka, PEE-ra ee-see-TEE-ree-ah yia tee see-nav-LEE-ah!
Έτσι, ρε μαλάκα, πήρα **εισιτήρια** για τη **συναυλία**!

Can he really say that on the radio?
Eh-pee-TREH-peh-teh na toh pee af-TOH stoh ra-thee-OH-foh-noh?
Επιτρέπεται να το πει αυτό στο **ραδιόφωνο**;

Do you play any instruments?
*PEH-zees Kah-NEH-nah **OR-gha-noh**?*
Παίζεις κανένα **όργανο**;

I used to play the guitar when I was a kid.
*EH-peh-za **kee-THAH-rah** OH-than EE-moon mee-KROHS.*
Έπαιζα **κιθάρα** όταν ήμουν μικρός.

My cousin plays bitchin' bouzouki.
*Oh KSA-ther-FOS moo PEH-zee gha-MAH- to **boo-ZOO-kee**.*
Ο ξάδερφός μου παίζει γαμάτο **μπουζούκι**.

The bouzouki is the traditional instrument of Greece. It's an acoustic stringed instrument with a bowl-shaped base. It has three or four sets of twin strings that produce a unique twang. You could call it a Greek banjo.

My neighbor's son plays his fucking drums all day.
*Oh yohs too YEE-toh-na PEH-zee ta gha-mee-MEH-na **drahms** too, OH-lee MEH-ra.*
Ο γιος του γείτονα παίζει τα γαμημένα **ντραμς** του, όλη μέρα.

I want to play the saxophone like Clinton.
*THEH-lo na PEH-zoh **sahx-OH-foh-noh** sahn tohn KLEE-ntohn.*
Θέλω να παίζω **σαξόφωνο** σαν τον Κλίντον.

····Greek music
Eh-lee-nee-KEE moo-see-KEE
Ελληνική μουσική

From old-school traditional to the more modern Greek pop, Greek music, like an elaborate tapestry, is woven deeply into the fabric of every citizen and ex-pat. Even the youngsters with the obnoxiously loud car stereos will sing along to the old, patriotic stuff. Below is some info on the major genres of Greek music, so you can keep up with the locals when the going gets ethnic.

Folk
La-ee-KA
Λαϊκά

This is some classic shit—the sound of the people. Just FYI, Greek folk music mainly focuses on good times, love, and politics. The third is covered elsewhere, but the first two fall into the realm of Λαϊκά. This is also the typical style of music that you'll find on a Best of Greece–type CD. All that cheesy, generic shit technically falls into this category. It's pop music, and just like we have the Beatles and the Bieber, there's good and bad of the Greek equivalent as well. One distinguishing characteristic about λαϊκή μουσική is that it covers both the modern and the traditional stuff. However, younger people do tend to refer to the new stuff as pop.

Pop
Pohp
Ποπ

Pop music in Greece is pretty much like pop music anywhere. It sucks, but most of it tends to be catchy enough. More specifically, pop refers to mainstream music that incorporates both traditional, bouzoukiish sounds along with more modern, electronic beats. The end result is a potpourri of shit most of the time, but its pop, so I guess that's par for the course.

Interpretative
EN-deh-hnee
Έντεχνη

You know that smooth acoustic stuff you might hear in a tea house or a spa? Well try to picture a more Middle Eastern version of that. The sound is very lute-heavy, accompanied by ethnic drums, and is usually quite relaxing and soothing. Think ethnic lounge.

Rebetika
Reh-BEH-tee-kah
Ρεμπέτικα

Dark, Middle Eastern beats and grungy bouzouki riffs, all accompanied with the rhythmic burble of a hookah in the background. Rebetika has been and always will be the music of the streets and their down-and-dirty inhabitants. Think Mediterranean blues here; these songs are about social turmoil, political injustice, and the sex and drugs used to numb them. Since the turn of the twentieth century, thieves, hippies, and revolutionaries have been vibing to rebetika from the speakeasy to the jail cell. Respect.

••••Foreign Music
XEH-na
Ξένα

One nice thing about Greek culture, as far as music goes, is that the youth of the country may get down to MTV's top-ten List, but they also know the stuff their grandparents listen to. We covered the Greek stuff; now it's time to look at the White Stripes, Tiesto, and Lady Gaga. Not too long ago, all music that did not involve a bouzouki was referred to as foreign (ξένα). Today's older fogies may still use this term, but the youngsters just call it music.

Rock
ROH-k
Ροκ

Sometimes you feel like you don't have a partner, and all you want to do is paint it black. But then you remember that you are a motherfuckin' voodoo child, and you love rock and roll! I could be wrong, but it seems that rock wins the popularity contest in Greece. This includes all types of rock from 80s hair bands to alternative to grunge. The Stones are huge, as are the White Stripes and the Black Keys. Metallica is God, and the Red Hot Chili Peppers are Jesus Christ. There are countless concerts with the biggest names, especially in the summer, and there are a million bars that rock out for the in-between time. It's surprising that the word ροκ is used almost exclusively for all rock subgenres, given the high level of rock knowledge that exists in the country.

Heavy metal
MEH-tal
Μέταλ

This is probably the only rock genre that is referred to exclusively by its name, most likely because most Greeks think metal sucks. A heavy metal fan is referred to, usually with at least some disdain, as a μεταλάς (*meh-tah-LAS*).

Techno
Ee-lek-troh-nee-KEE moo-see-KEE
Ηλεκρονική μουσική

Eminem once said that no one listens to techno. Clearly that little white boy never made his way to Mykonos or Agia Napa. Just like soccer and Formula 1, electronic music is much more popular everywhere but the States, and it particularly enjoys a strong following on the Greek peninsula. In the summer months, the world's who's who of DJs, including the likes of Tiesto, Tomcraft, and Oakenfold, grace the country's beachside clubs, and in the winter they make their way to Athens's warehouses. If you've ever stuck your head into the heroin-chic world of synthesized music, you'll know that: (1) the girls are stupid hot, and (2) there is a virtual shitstorm of electronic subgenres, all of which are separated by no more than a beat, pop, or a bang. Here's a quick description of the main techno genres Greek's slap in their tuned French and German cars.

House
HA-oos
Χάουζ

Greeks use the word "house" the way we use the word "techno," as a broad descriptive term for the entire genre. It technically only applies to the more generic, intense, fast-paced, but not overwhelming "techno" sound that every idiot puts on their street-racing videos on YouTube.

Trance
Trans
Τρανς

This is the heavy shit. You know what I'm talking about. You either love it or you hate it, and even if it's the former, you really have to be in the mood for it. The locals call this stuff τα πριόνια (the chain saws). Fitting, if you ask me.

Lounge
LAH-oondz
Λάουντζ

Every trendy café in Athens plays a continuous stream of lounge music day and night, 24/7. This is basically techno for when you just can't handle anymore techno. If you're not sure what sound I'm talking about just look up Café Del Mar on YouTube. There's like 47 of these albums, kind of like the countless Now That's What I Call Music—just actually listenable.

Hip-Hop
Heep-HOHP
Χιπ-Χοπ

The rap and hip-hop scene in Greece is brand-new, by which I mean it still kinda sucks. Just two years ago, Greeks were introduced to 50 Cent, Eminem, Beyoncé, and that really was it. It's growing rapidly in popularity but will never really be quite mainstream, and it definitely won't take over as the club music of choice, but you can hear some good slap if you know where to look. There are a few promotional party groups, mainly made up of Greek-American kids who throw some slammin' hip-hop parties on select nights in the city's best clubs. Just check online for any Mad GQ, Urban Vibe, or Magna parties.

THE TOOLS OF THE TRADE)))
TAH ER-GHA-LEE-AH
ΤΑ ΕΡΓΑΛΕΙΑ

Are you really still rocking a **Walkman**?
*Ah-KOH-ma meh toh **WAHK-mahn**, re-SEE?*
Ακόμα με το **γουόκμαν**, ρε συ;

I'm on the waiting list for the new **iPod**.
*EE-meh seh LEES-ta yia toh keh-NOOR-yoh **AHEE-pohd**.*
Είμαι σε λίστα για το καινούργιο **iPod**.

This is a good example of some of the rare cases when a word is either so brand-oriented or too cumbersome to write phonetically in Greek that it will actually be written in English or, more specifically, Latin characters.

Let me borrow your **headphones**.
*THA-nee-SEH moo ta **ah-koo-stee-KA** soo.*
Δάνεισέ μου τα **ακουστικά** σου.

I think I just blew out my **speakers**.
*Noh-MEE-zoh pohs MO-lees EH-kah-psah ta **EE-hee-ah** moo.*
Νομίζω πως μόλις έκαψα τα **ηχεία** μου.

I'm going to install this **amp** and my shit is going to **pound**!
*Thah VA-lo af-TOH tohn **eh-nee-shee-TEE** keh thah **vah-RAH-ee** toh SEES-stee-mah!*
Θα βάλω αυτό τον **ενισχυτή** και θα **βαράει** το σύστημα!

••••TV
Tee-le-OH-ra-see
Τηλεόραση

What's on the **idiot box**?
*Tee Eh-heeh toh **hah-zoh-KOO-tee**?*
Τι έχει το **χαζοκούτι**;

Pass me the remote.
THO-seh moo toh kohn-TROL.
Δώσε μου το **κοντρόλ**.

Scoot over, my show is starting.
KA-neh AH-kree, ar-HEE-zee ee see-RAH moo.
Κάνε άκρη, αρχίζει η **σειρά** μου.

Did you record the game?
EH-ghra-psess toh mats?
Έγραψες το ματς;

••••Movies
The-NEE-ess
Ταινίες

Let's go to the movies.
PA-meh see-neh-MA.
Πάμε **σινεμά**.

You know what's weird about the movies in Greece? Assigned seating.

Can you get me a ticket?
Boh-REES na moo PAH-rees ee-see-TEE-ree-oh?
Μπορείς να μου πάρεις **εισιτήριο**;

What film are we going to see?
Pyo ER-gho tha THOO-meh?
Ποιο **έργο** θα δούμε;

I hope it's not dubbed and there are subtitles.
El-PEE-zoh na meen EE-neh meh-tah-ghlo-teez-MEH-noh ken na EH-hee ee-POH-tee-tloos.
Ελπίζω να μην είναι **μεταγλωττισμένο**και να έχει **υπότιτλους**.

Let's go see a/an...flick.
PAH-meh nah DOO-meh MEE-ah...teh-NEE-ah
Πάμε να δούμε μία...ταινία

> comedy
> *koh-moh-DEE-ah*
> κωμωδία

drama
drah-mah-tee-KEE
δραματική

action
DRAH-sees
δράσης

chick flick
eh-sthee-mah-tee-KEE
αισθηματική

cartoon
kar-TOON
καρτούν

••••The cell phone
Toh kee-nee-TOH
Το κινητό

I first saw what a text message was in Greece. My first color screen was old there before it was new in the U.S. My Greek Sony Ericsson flip phone was so clean I wanted to cry, and I did when I found out that it wasn't available here. A classmate said once that cell phone usage in Greece was over 90 percent, so say 85 percent to be safe and that's still an impressive figure. More impressive than that is seeing how much of a fashion accessory the phone is. Everybody—and I mean everybody—takes their cell out of their pocket and puts it on the table at a café, bar, or restaurant. They say it's for comfort reasons, and the tight-ass Euro jeans may back this up, but don't buy it. It's bullshit.

I forgot my **cell phone** in the car.
*KSEH-ha-sa toh **kee-nee-TOH** moo stoh ah-MA-ksee.*
Ξέχασα το **κινητό** μου στο αμάξι.

Call me back, I'm almost out of **minutes**.
*PA-reh meh Eh-SEE, then EH-hoh AH-less **moh-NAH-thes**.*
Πάρε με εσύ, δεν έχω άλλες **μονάδες**.

I'll give you a **missed call** when I get there.
*Tha soo KA-noh **ah-na-PAHN-dee-tee** OH-than FTA-soh.*
Θα σου κάνω **αναπάντητη** όταν φτάσω.

I've only seen this in Greece: Instead of texting, you call and hang up after one ring. Great for telling someone you're waiting in the car.

Text me, I can't hear you.
*Then sa-KOO-oh, STEE-leh moo **MEE-nee-mah**.*
Δεν σ' ακούω, στείλε μου **μήνυμα**.

Give me your **charger**, because my **battery** is dead.
*FEH-reh moo toh **for-tee-STEE** soo, yia-TEE TA-hee PEH-ksee ee **bah-ta-REE-ah** moo.*
Φέρε μου το **φορτιστή** σου, γιατί τα 'χει παίξει η **μπαταρία** μου.

••••Computers
EE-poh-loh-yee-STES
Υπολογιστές

Most of the computer-related vocab in Greece is ripped straight from English. Here are the ones that have Greek names, but even they are used interchangeably with their English counterparts.

I haven't **downloaded** any unzipping **program** yet.
*Then EH-hoh **kah-the-VAH-see** kah-NEH-nah **PROH-ghra-ma** yia ahn-ZEE-peeng ah-KOH-mah.*
Δεν έχω **κατεβάσει** κανένα **πρόγραμα** για ανζίπινγκ ακόμα.

Holy shit, I don't think I saved the **file**.
*Po, reh POOS-tee, then noh-MEE-zoh oh-TEE EH-soh-sah toh **ar-HEE-oh**.*
Πω, ρε πούστη, δεν νομίζω ότι έσωσα το **αρχείο**.

My **laptop**'s speakers are shit.
*Tah ee-HEE-ah too **LAHP-tohp** moo EE-neh yia tohn POO-tsoh.*
Τα ηχεία του **λάπτοπ** μου είναι για τον πούτσο.

I think my **computer** has one hell of a **virus**.
*Noh-MEE-zoh OH-tee oh **ee-poh-loh-yee-STEES** moo EH-hee var-VA-tee **EE-oh-see**.*
Νομίζω ότι ο **υπολογιστής** μου έχει βαρβάτη **ίωση**.

You can say "computer" and "virus" just as often as you use the Greek words.

I was a little drunk and spilled half my drink into my **keyboard**.
*EE-moon-ah Psee-loh-meh-thee-ZMEH-nohs k-EH-reek-sa toh poh-TOH moo stoh **pleek-troh-LOH-yee-oh**.*
Ήμουν ψιλομεθυσμένος και έριξα το ποτό μου στο **πληκτρολόγιο**.

I forgot to get paper for the **printer**.
*KSEH-ha-sa na PA-roh har-TEE yia tohn **ek-tee-poh-TEE**.*
Ξέχασα να πάρω χαρτί για τον **εκτυπωτή**.

I wish I had a **cordless mouse**.
*Mah-KAH-ree na EE-ha **ah-SEER-ma-toh poh-DEE-kee**.*
Μακάρι να είχα **ασύρματο ποντίκι**.

Dude, all my shit is **pirated**.
*Reh ma-LA-ka, OH-lee moo ee see-loh-GEE EE-neh **pee-ra-tee-KEE**.*
Ρε μαλάκα, όλη μου η συλλογή είναι **πειρατική**.

Tell me that website again.
*XA-na-PEZ moo teen **ee-stoh-seh-LEE-tha**.*
Ξαναπές μου την **ιστοσελίδα**.

I find all my ass on the Internet.
*VREE-skoh tah PAH-dah stoh **IN-ter-net**.*
Βρίσκω τα πάντα στο **ίντερνετ**.

····Shorthand
See-ntoh-moh-grah-FEE-ah
Συντομογραφία

People are lazy the world over, and this is no more evident than by taking a look at how we txt—sorry text. Every language has its own SMS language complete with an alphabet, and Greek is no exception. Here's a few of the most popular ones.

MLK
ΜΛΚ
No, not Martin Luther King, but rather the world-famous and much loved μαλάκα (asshole).

LOL
LOL
Don't really need to explain this one, and if I do, then you're probably a little too old for this book.

DLD
ΔΛΔ
Short for δηλαδή (*thee-la-THEE*). It can either mean "because" or "meaning…?"

TPT
ΤΠΤ
Short for τίποτα (*TEE-poh-ta*), which means "nothing."

Χαχαχα
Χαχαχα
The Greek version of "hahaha."

KTL

ΚΤΛ

This is a good one. It's short for και τα λοιπά (*ke tah lee-PAH*) which is "etcetera" in Greek.

MNM

MNM

Short for μήνυμα (*MEE-nee-mah*) which means "message." Mostly used in text messaging on cell phones.

····Fashion
EE MOH-dah
Η μόδα

Maybe when you think about the Greek way of dressing, chitons and sandals come to mind, just like ancient Greeks wore. Things have changed quite a bit! Young people in Greece adopt the same style as the Americans (but with about a one-year delay). Women take care of themselves and you'll find them dressed up and wearing make-up for every occasion. Men prefer a more casual look, mostly jeans and T-shirts. Their formal but still trendy getup is not so different from their usual outfit: blue jeans, white shirt, black shoes.

That dress fits you very well!
Af-toh to FOH-re-mah sou PAH-ee poh-LEE!
Αυτό το **φόρεμα** σου πάει πολύ!

I prefer skinny jeans over baggy ones.
Pro-tee-MOH ta steh-NA apoh tah far-dee-AH geen.
Προτιμώ τα στενά από τα φαρδιά **τζιν**.

That guy is super-trendy.
Af-tohs o TEE-pohs EE-neh poh-LEE TREHN-dee.
Αυτός ο τύπος είναι πολύ **τρέντι**.
It leaves a sense of sarcasm, though.

CHAPTER 8

SPORTY GREEK

AH-THLEE-TEE-KA EH-LEE-NEE-KA
Αθλητικά Ελληνικά

From basketball to wrestling sans toga, the Greeks have been ballin' since way back in the day, and they are no strangers to a little athletic competition. After all, they invented the goddamn Olympics! So, credit where credit is due. Soccer is the number one spectator sport, but the Greeks are heavy into basketball as well, having proven themselves on the European and world stages on more than one occasion. Summertime is all about watersports, and there's even a rapidly growing group of skiers, snowboarders, and all around snow junkies. The street-racing scene is always hot for you true delinquents and speed freaks out there.

····Sports
Ah-thlee-tee-KA
Αθλητικά

"Healthy mind, healthy body." (*Noos ee-YEEIS en SOH-ma-tee ee-YEEI*; νους υγιής εν σώματι υγιεί.) The ancients knew what they were talking about. A healthy mind is an important thing to have, but the body that it holds needs to be taken care of as well.

Do you follow any sports?
*Ahs-hoh-LEE-seh meh ta **ath-lee-tee-KA**?*
Ασχολείσαι με τα **αθλητικά**;

You play any sports?
PEH-zees KA-na spor?
Παίζεις κάνα **σπορ**;

Which do you like more, soccer or basketball?
*Tee ghoo-STA-rees peh-ree-SOH-the-roh, **BAH-la** ee **BAHS-ket**?*
Τι γουστάρεις περισσότερο, **μπάλα** ή **μπάσκετ**;

Μπάλα means "ball," but it implies soccer in this popular phrase. It sort of implies the number one spot in popularity that soccer occupies in both Greece and most of the world.

What's your team?
*Tee **oh-MA-tha** EE-seh?*
Τι **ομάδα** είσαι;

The top three teams in Greece are Ολυμπιακός (*oh-leem-pee-ah-KOS*), Παναθηναϊκός (*pa-na-thee-na-ee-KOS*), and ΑΕΚ (*AH-ek*).

I used to play when I was young.
EH-peh-za mee-KROS.
Έπαιζα μικρός.

Let's go see a game one of these days.
*PA-meh na THOO-meh EH-na **mats** ka-MYA MEH-ra.*
Πάμε να δούμε ένα **ματς** καμιά μέρα.

All the hooligans went downtown and fucked shit up.
*YEH-mee-seh toh KE-droh **HOO-lee-gan** ke **toh KA-na-neh moo-NEE**.*
Γέμισε όλο το κέντρο **χούλιγκαν** και **το κάνανε μουνί**.
Every team has a fringe following of violent fans that enjoy the fight as much as the game itself. Many times the fight makes its way from the stadium to downtown Athens.

What time is the national team playing?
*Tee OH-rah PEH-zee ee **eth-nee-KEE**?*
Τι ώρα παίζει η **εθνική**;

Are they going to show the final at the bar?
*Tha THEE-xoon tohn **teh-lee-KO** stoh bahr?*
Θα δείξουν τον **τελικό** στο μπαρ;

Fuck those fucking refs!
Gha-MOH tee thyeh-tee-SEE-ah moo gha-MOH!
Γαμώ τη διαιτησία μου, γαμώ!
This way of drawing attention to bad call-making.

What's the score?
POH-sa?
Πόσα;

This game's a fucking blowout.
Peh-HNEE-thee EE TSON-da VLEH-poo-meh?
Παιχνίδι ή τσόντα βλέπουμε;
Literally, "Are we watching a game or a porno?"

····Soccer
Poh-THOH-sfe-roh
Ποδόσφαιρο

Soccer is king the world over, and Greece is no exception. The Greek league is strong, but not quite up to the level of the powerhouse English, Spanish, and Italian leagues that dominate European competition. Be that as it may, the top Greek teams like Olympiakos and Panathinaikos are world-class, and they can go toe to toe with the best the world has to offer any day.

Who's your favorite…?

Pyos EE-neh oh ah-gha-pee-MEH-nos soo…?

Ποιος είναι ο αγαπημένος σου...;

forward
fohr
φορ

striker
SEH-der fohr
σέντερ φορ

midfielder
MEH-soss
μέσος

defender
ah-mee-dee-KOS
αμυντικός

sweeper
ke-dree-KOS ah-mee-dee-KOS
κεντρικός αμυντικός

goalie
ter-ma-toh-FEE-la-kas
τερματοφύλακας

coach
proh-po-nee-TEES
προπονητής

ref
thy-eh-tee-TEES
διαιτητής

Who's leading the **championship**?

*Pyos EE-neh PROH-tos stoh **proh-TA-thlee-ma**?*

Ποιος είναι πρώτος στο **πρωτάθλημα**;

Goal!!!!

Gohl, gha-moh teen poo-TA-na moo!!!!

Γκολ, γαμώ την πουτάνα μου!!!

Where were they offside!?
POO EE-neh toh ohf-SA-eed!?
Πού είναι το **οφσάιντ**;
Bad offside calls are a favorite topic of the Monday morning coaches.

There's a Champion's League game on Wednesday.
EH-hee TSAM-pee-ons leeg teen teh-TAR-tee.
Έχει **Τσάμπιονς Λιγκ** την Τετάρτη.

Tomorrow's game is going to be a close contest.
Toh av-ree-ah-NOH mats tha EE-neh DER-bee.
Το αυριανό ματς θα είναι **ντέρμπι**.

Did you see the dribble that son of a bitch just pulled off?
EE-thes MEE-ah TREE-plah poo EH-kah-neh oh POOS-tees?
Είδες μια **τρίπλα** που έκανε ο πούστης;

He took apart their entire defense.
Toos AH-nee-xeh OH-lee teen AH-mee-na.
Τους άνοιξε όλη την **άμυνα**.

If extra time ends in a tie, they'll go to a penalty shootout.
AH-ma te-lee-OH-see ee-so-pa-LEE-ah ee pa-RA-ta-see, tha PA-meh sta PEH-nal-tee.
Άμα τελειώσει ισοπαλία η **παράταση**, θα πάμε στα **πέναλτι**.

Olympiakos's starting 11 is very strong this year.
EE-neh poh-LEE yeh-REE ee en-te-KA-tha too oh-leem-bee-ah-KOO FEH-tohs.
Είναι πολύ γερή η **εντεκάδα** του Ολυμπιακού φέτος.

····Basketball
BAH-sket
Μπάσκετ

Greece is better at basketball than they are at soccer, having had much more success in European and international competition. Ever heard of Greek Baby Shaq? Google it.

Number 15 has a really good **three pointer**.
*EH-hee ka-LOH **TREE-pon-doh** toh the-kaPEN-deh.*
Έχει καλό **τρίποντο** το δεκαπέντε.

He missed the **slam dunk**!
*Then TOO-kah-tse toh **SLAHM dahnk**!*
Δεν του 'κατσε το **σλαμ ντανκ**!

They called **traveling**.
*SFEE-ree-xane **VEE-ma-ta**.*
Σφύριξαν **βήματα**.

Do you follow the NBA at all?
Pa-ra-koh-loo-THAS ka-THOH-loo en-bee-EHEE?
Παρακολουθάς καθόλου NBA;

Basketball fans in Greece love their European leagues, but they know the best ball is still played Stateside.

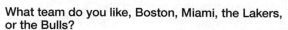

What team do you like, Boston, Miami, the Lakers, or the Bulls?
Py-AH oh-MA-tha soo ah-REH-see, ee Vos-TOH-nee, toh Maee-AH-mee, ee LEHEE-kers ee ee Bools?
Ποια ομάδα σου αρέσει, η Βοστώνη, το Μαϊάμι, οι Λέικερς ή οι Μπουλς;

Every Greek loves Michael Jordan, so most die-hards still tend to support the Bulls. Miami is a close second.

The **Eurobasket championship** is ours this year.
*EE-neh thee-KOH mas FEH-tos toh **Ev-roh-BAHS-ket**.*
Είναι δικό μας φέτος το **Ευρωμπάσκετ**.

Are you watching the **playoffs**?
*VLEH-pees **PLEHEE-ohf**?*
Βλέπεις **πλέιοφ**;

He's not missing both **free throws**.
*Then PEH-zee na HA-see ke tees THEE-oh **voh-LES**.*
Δεν παίζει να χάσει και τις δύο **βολές**.

····The Olympics
Ee oh-leem-bee-ah-KEE ah-YHO-nes
Οι Ολυμπιακοί Αγώνες

Where are the next **Olympics** going to be held?
*Poo thah EE-neh ee eh-POH-meh-nee **oh-leem-bee-AH-tha**?*
Πού θα είναι η επόμενη **Ολυμπιάδα**;

I really like **track and field**, especially the **100-meter dash**.
*Moo ah-REH-see oh **STEE-vos** poh-LEE, kee-REE-os ta **eh-ka-TOH MEH-tra**.*
Μου αρέσει ο **στίβος** πολύ, κυρίως τα **εκατό μέτρα**.

I can't believe it, we got the **gold medal**!
*Then toh pees-TEV-oh, PEE-ra-meh toh **hree-SOH meh-TA-lee-oh**!*
Δεν το πιστεύω, πήραμε το **χρυσό μετάλλιο**!

All the **swimmers** look like they're **doping**.
*OH-lee ee **koh-leem-vee-TES** EE-neh **doh-pa-reez-MEH-nee**.*
Όλοι οι **κολυμβητές** είναι **ντοπαρισμένοι**.

We just own in **weightlifting**.
*Ah-PLOS gha-MA-meh steen **AR-see va-RON**.*
Απλώς γαμάμε στην **άρση βαρών**.

I'm going to the **velodrome** to watch the **cycling**.
*PA-oh sto **poh-dee-lah-toh-DRO-meeo** na thoh **poh-thee-la-SEE-ah**.*
Πάω στο **ποδηλατοδρόμιο** να δω **ποδηλασία**.

I'm not going to sit and watch fucking **gymnastics**.
*Then KA-thoh-meh na tho ko-lo **koh-loh-eh-NOH-rgah-nee**.*
Δεν κάθομαι να δω **κωλο-ενόργανη**.

I usually don't watch the winter games.
See-NEE-thos then VLEH-poh toos hee-meh-ree-NOOS ah-YHO-nes.
Συνήθως δεν βλέπω τους **χειμερινούς αγώνες**.

I only like the figure skating.
MOH-noh toh pa-tee-NAZ moo ah-REH-see.
Μόνο το **πατινάζ** μου αρέσει.

····Other sports
AH-la ath-LEE-ma-ta
Άλλα αθλήματα

Tennis is a little too rich for my blood.
Toh TEH-nees EE-neh poh-LEE kee-ree-LEH yia teen PAR-tee moo.
Το **τένις** είναι πολύ κυριλέ για την πάρτη μου.

The funny thing is that I know quite a few people who do horseback riding.
EE PLA-ka EE-neh oh-TEE XEH-roh ar-ke-TA AH-toh-ma poo KA-noon ee-pa-SEE-ah.
Η πλάκα είναι ότι ξέρω αρκετά άτομα που κάνουν **ιππασία**.

Equestrian sports actually enjoy a decent following in Greece, and there has been some Olympic success as a result of it.

I'm going skiing at Mt. Parnassus.
PA-oh stohn Par-na-SOH na KA-noh skee.
Πάω στον Παρνασσό να κάνω **σκι**.

Mount Parnassus is THE spot for skiing, snowboarding, or chasing snow bunnies.

What am I middle-aged!? Of course I prefer snowboarding.
Mes-EE-lee-kas EE-meh!? Fee-see-KA proh-tee-moh toh snohoo-BORD.
Μεσήλικας είμαι; Φυσικά προτιμώ το **σνοουμπόρντ**.

You do any sort of fighting?
*PEH-zees ka-NA **XEE-loh**?*
Παίζεις κανα **ξύλο**;
Ξύλο means "wood." Yeah, it's weird.

I like kickboxing and muay thai.
*Moo ah-REH-soon toh **KEEK-bohx** ke toh **MA-ee-TA-ee**.*
Μου αρέσουν το **κικ μποξ** και το **μάι τάι**.
Martial arts are very popular, especially these two.

Bowling is for pussies.
*Toh **BOHOO-leeng** EE-neh yia FLOH-roos.*
Το **μπόουλινγκ** είναι για φλώρους.

I've spent semesters playing pool.
*EH-hoh peh-RA-see TREE-mee-na stoh **beel-YAR-thoh**.*
Έχω περάσει τρίμηνα στο **μπιλιάρδο**.

Do you play cards?
PEH-zees har-TYA?
Παίζεις χαρτιά;

> **Blackjack**
> *Ee-koh-see EH-na*
> Εικοσιένα
> Literally, "twenty-one."

> **Poker**
> *POH-ker*
> Πόκερ

> **Solitaire**
> *Pas-IEN-tza*
> Πασιέντζα

> **Biriba**
> *Bee-REE-ba*
> Μπιρίμπα
> *Biriba* is an old Greek card game similar to rummy, and it's extremely popular with all ages. It's a good cultural skill to have up your sleeve. If you want to learn, you can find pretty solid instructions at www.biribagame.com.

····Dance
Hoh-ROS
Χορός

I just can't date a dancer.
*Poh-LEE ah-PLA, then boh-ROH na ta EH-hoh meh **hoh-REH-ftree-ah**.*
Πολύ απλά δεν μπορώ να τα έχω με **χορεύτρια**.

Do you wanna dance?
*THEH-lees na **hoh-REH-psoo-meh**?*
Θέλεις να **χορέψουμε**;

I really like this song.
Moo ah-REH-see poh-LEE af-toh toh tra-YHOO-thee.
Μου αρέσει πολύ αυτό το τραγούδι.

Want us to learn ballet?
*THEH-lees na MA-thoo-meh **ba-LE-toh**?*
Θέλεις να μάθουμε **μπαλέτο**;

Hip-hop is actually really good exercise.
*PLA-ka PLA-ka, toh **HEEP hohp** EE-neh poh-LEE ka-LEE yee-mna-stee-KEE.*
Πλάκα πλάκα, το **χιπ χοπ** είναι είναι πολύ καλή γυμναστική.

Hip-hop and Latin are the two most popular forms of dancing that the Greek public partakes in, whether it's in a dance studio or a club.

Just know salsa and you're good.
***SAL-sa** na XEH-rees keh EE-seh koh-BLE.*
Σάλσα να ξέρεις και είσαι κομπλέ.

Folk dancing bores me to tears.
*Var-YEH-meh ah-FAN-da-sta toos **pa-ra-thoh-see-ah-KOOS hoh-ROOS**.*
Βαριέμαι αφάνταστα τους **παραδοσιακούς χορούς**.

You'll see Greeks dancing in circles during every important celebration, like weddings, birthdays, and christenings, but also at the clubs.

I'll give you a **lap dance** at the house if you behave
yourself.
*Tha soo KA-noh EH-na **streep-TEEZ** stoh SPEE-tee, AH-
ma EE-seh FROH-nee-mos.*
Θα σου κάνω ένα **στριπτίζ** στο σπίτι, άμα είσαι
φρόνιμος.

····Motorsports
Ah-YHO-nes mee-hah-noh-KEE-nee-sees
Αγώνες μηχανοκίνησης

Those **Formula 1** drivers make crazy money.
*VGHA-zoon treh-LA lef-TA ee oh-thee-YEE tees **FOHR-
myoo-la EH-na**.*
Βγάζουν τρελά λεφτά οι οδηγοί της **Φόρμουλα Ένα**.

Formula 1 is the premier level of auto racing and is second only
to soccer in worldwide popularity.

I'm going to go see the **Acropolis Rally** in person
this year.
*Tha PA-oh na thoh toh **RA-lee ah-KROH-poh-lees** LA-
eev FEH-tos.*
Θα πάω να δω το **Ράλι Ακρόπολις** λάιβ φέτος.

The Acropolis Rally is one of the most important races on the
World Rally Championship calendar every year and is one of the
country's most popular touristic attractions.

STREET-RACING)))

KOHN-DRES
ΚΟΝΤΡΕΣ

Street-racing is big throughout the entire country. Make your way to one of the many popular racing spots if you have a need for speed.

Let's go to the seaside to watch the street-racing.
*PA-meh lee-ma-NA-kya na THOO-meh tees **KOHN-dres**.*
Πάμε Λιμανάκια να δούμε τις **κόντρες**.

That car is tricked the fuck out.
EE-neh koh-loh-ftyagh-MEH-noh toh ah-MA-xee.
Είναι κωλοφτιαγμένο το αμάξι.

Dude, that M3 is fast as balls.
*Ma-LA-ka, **PA-ee tohn KOH-loh too** toh mee-TREE-ah.*
Μαλάκα, **πάει τον** κώλο του το M3.

Motherfucker took that turn sideways.
BEE-keh meh tees PAH-ndes tohn gha-mee-MEH-noh.
Μπήκε με τις πάντες το γαμημένο.

Careful, he's got a turbo.
*PROH-seh-heh, EE-neh **toor-BA-tos**.*
Πρόσεχε, είναι **τουρμπάτος**.
Or you could just say TOOR-boh.

Is your bike a 600 or a 1.000?
*Tee EE-neh ee **mee-ha-NEE** soo, eh-xa-koh-SA-ra EE heel-YA-ra?*
Τι είναι η **μηχανή** σου, εξακοσάρα ή χιλιάρα;

It rips wheelies like no other.
***Soo-ZA-ree** ya tohn POO-tsoh too.*
Σουζάρει για τον πούτσο του.
A wheelie is called a σούζα [SOO-za].

Put a helmet on before you kill yourself.
*VA-leh **KRA-nos** preen skoh-toh-THEES.*
Βάλε **κράνος** πριν σκοτωθείς.

Rossi is a MotoGP boss.

*Oh ROH-see EE-neh oh AR-hoh-ndas too **MOH-toh-dzee-pee***.

Ο Ρόσι είναι ο άρχοντας του **Μότο GP**.

There is no rider more popular than Valentino "The Doctor" Rossi.

····The gym
Toh yee-mna-STEE-ree-oh
Το γυμναστήριο

Most people aren't born with it, so the gyms get a lot of business in Greece. One can't afford to be spilling out of one's bathing suit in this beach-going, sunbathing country.

Where is/are...?
POO EE-neh toh/tah...?
Πού είναι το/τα..;

the gym
toh yee-mna-STEE-ree-oh

το γυμναστήριο

the free-weights
tah VAH-ree/tah vah-RA-kya

τα βάρη/τα βαράκια

Use βάρη for the bigger free-weights and βαράκια for the lighter dumbells.

the locker room
tah ah-poh-thee-TEE-ree-ah

τα αποδυτήρια

You might have noticed that this word is plural, so you would at a τα in front if you wanted to say "the locker room."

the pool
ee pee-SEE-na

η πισίνα

You Spanish speakers should recognize this word. Yup, the Greeks invented that too!

the exercise bike

Sta-theh-ROH poh-THEE-la-toh

σταθερό ποδήλατο

Literally, stationary bicycle. If you're at the gym already, you can just say "ποδήλατο."

the StairMaster

SKA-less

σκάλες

You're just saying "stairs" here.

I'm thinking about doing **personal training**.

*LEH-oh na KA-noh **PEHR-sohn-al TREH-ee-neeng**.*

Λέω να κάνω **πέρσοναλ τρέινινγκ**.

Today, I'm going to focus on my **abs** and **chest**.

*SEE-meh-ra tha KA-noh **kee-lee-ah-KOOS** keh **STEE-thohs**.*

Σήμερα θα κάνω **κοιλιακούς** και **στήθος**.

Show me one person who likes the **treadmill**.

*THEE-xeh moo EH-nan AN-throh-poh poo too ah-REH-see oh **THYA-throh-mohs**.*

Δείξε μου έναν άνθρωπο που του αρέσει ο **διάδρομος**.

How much weight did you put on the bar?

POH-sa KEE-la EH-va-less steen BA-ra?

Πόσα κιλά έβαλες στην μπάρα;

This is a very important question to be able to ask in your spotter's native tongue.

I'm going to the **steam room** to loosen up.

*PA-oh stee **SA-oo-na** na hah-lah-ROH-soh.*

Πάω στη **σάουνα** να χαλαρώσω.

I never **warm up** before I work out.

*Then KA-noh po-TE **pro-THER-mahn-see**.*

Δεν κάνω ποτέ **προθέρμανση**.

I go to the gym at night because there's more tail then.

Pee-YEH-no ya yee-mna-stee-KEE ta VRA-thya, ya-TEE PE-zee py-OH po-LEE moo-NEE.

Πηγαίνω για γυμναστική τα βράδια, γιατί παίζει πιο πολύ μουνί.

Did you stretch first?

*EH-ka-ness **STREH-tseeng** PROH-ta?*

Έκανες **στρέτσινγκ** πρώτα;

Nope…

CHAPTER NINE

HUNGRY GREEK

PEE-NAZ-MEH-NA EH-LEE-NEE-KA

Πεινασμένα Ελληνικά

The food. Oh my God, the food. First of all, the fruits and vegetables actually taste and smell like fruits and vegetables. Crazy, I know. And you haven't tasted a gyro until you've had one in Syntagma Square. They're insane. The seafood is mind-numbingly good too. One trip to a fish tavern and you'll be struck by the realization that you've never really liked seafood because the fishsticks you nuke at home ain't worth shit. No doubt there's an abundance of good eats in Greece, but the best part by far is that you can get a decent amount of it at any time. Thin-crust Italian pizza or an orgasm-inducing crêpe at four in the morning? Sold. There is no finer way to prevent the night's tequila from making a comeback.

····Hungry
PEE-na
Πείνα

Are you hungry?
Pee-NAS?
Πεινάς;

What kinda food we got?
Ah-POH fa-EE tee PEH-zee?
Από **φαΐ** τι παίζει;

Have you eaten anything today?
EH-hees FA-ee TEE-poh-ta SEE-meh-ra?
Έχεις φάει τίποτα σήμερα;

I'm kind of hungry.
Psee-loh-pee-NA-oh.
Ψιλοπεινάω.

I'm starving!
EH-hoh peh-THA-nee steen PEE-na!
'Εχω πεθάνει στην πείνα!

What are we eating?
Tee TROH-meh?
Τι **τρώμε**;

I'm not cooking shit!
Then ma-yee-REH-voh TEE-poh-ta!
Δεν **μαγειρεύω** τίποτα!

I'm thinking about ordering some food. You want anything?
LEH-oh na pa-ra-GEE-loh. Thehs TEE-poh-ta?
Λέω να **παραγγείλω**. Θες τίποτα;

I didn't have time to eat...
Then PROH-la-va na FA-oh...
Δεν πρόλαβα να **φάω**...

> **breakfast.**
> *proh-ee-NOH.*
> πρωινό.

lunch.
meh-see-mer-ya-NOH.
μεσημεριανό.

dinner.
vra-thee-NOH.
βραδινό.

a snack.
KA-na bee-neh-LEE-kee.
κάνα μπινελίκι.

I want something sweet.
THEH-loh KA-tee ylee-KOH.
Θέλω κάτι **γλυκό**.

I just need to snack on something before I pass out.
Ah-PLA na tsee-BEE-soh KA-tee preen lee-poh-theeh-MEE-soh.
Απλώς να **τσιμπήσω** κάτι πριν λιποθυμήσω.

I just stuffed my face.
MOH-lees pla-KOH-theeh-ka sto fa-YEE-toh.
Μόλις πλακώθηκα στο φαγητό.

I'm not hungry.
Then pee-NA-oh.
Δεν πεινάω.

····Thirsty
THEE-psa
Δίψα

I'm thirsty.
Thee-PSA-oh.
Διψάω.

Do you want something to drink?
THEH-lees KA-tee na py-EES?
Θέλεις κάτι να **πιεις**;

Get me...
VA-leh moo...
Βάλε μου...

a glass of **water**.
*EH-na poh-TEE-ree **neh-ROH**.*
ένα ποτήρι **νερό**.

a cup of **coffee**.
*EH-nan **ka-FE**.*
έναν **καφέ**.

a Greek coffee.
EH-nahn Eh-lee-nee-KO.
έναν Ελληνικό.
Greek coffee is just like Arabic coffee, minus the cardamom.

a frappé.
EH-na fra-PEH.
ένα φραπέ.
The world-famous Greek Φραπέ is Nescafé instant coffee whipped with sugar and cold water, poured over ice, and topped off with evaporated milk. It was invented in Greece in the 50s, and there's no denying its superstar status in Greek coffee-drinking culture. It goes great with a cigarette, another national pastime.

a fréddo.
EH-na FREH-doh.
ένα φρέντο.
A fréddo is either a cold cappuccino or espresso. Another Greek concoction, both varieties are stupid good. If you like coffee, you'll definitely get off on these. Think of them as the frappé's grown-up cousin.

a cup of tea.
MEE-ah KOO-pa TSA-ee.
μία κούπα τσάι.

a soda.
EH-na ah-na-pseek-tee-KO.
ένα αναψυκτικό.

some juice.
LEE-gho hee-MOH.
λίγο χυμό.

a glass of milk.
EH-na poh-TEE-ree GHA-la.
ένα ποτήρι γάλα.

a beer.
MEE-ah BEE-ra.
μία μπίρα.

a drink.
EH-na poh-TOH.
ένα ποτό.
By "drink," I mean alcohol.

····Food
Fa-yee-TOH
Φαγητό

Anywhere you go in Greece, the food is fucking amazing. Just accept this as fact and keep reading. There's ton's of grilled meat and fish, as well as many raw and cooked vegetables. Rice, pasta, and pies are pretty common, but bread is the number one starch in the Greek diet. They eat an obscene amount of it! There is also one hell of a selection of sweet and savory phyllo-based pies. The funny thing is that everything tastes amazing, but it's pretty much all good for you, and even though the Greeks do it backwards and eat a shit-ton late at night, they still stay pretty healthy.

Let's go get some **gyros**.
*PA-meh yah **soo-VLA-kya**.*
Πάμε για **σουβλάκια**.

Gyros are actually called σουβλάκια (*soo-VLA-kya*) in Athens, but they're still referred to as γύρο (*YEE-roh*) everywhere else.

Dude, I just ate 12 shish kebabs.

*Ma-LA-ka, MOH-lees EH-fa-yha THOH-theh-ka **ka-la-MA-kya**.*

Μαλάκα, μόλις έφαγα δώδεκα **καλαμάκια**.

So the problems carry on. Shish kebabs are called σουβλάκια (*soo-VLA-kya*) all over Greece except for the capitol, where they are called καλαμάκια. This and the γύρο discrepancy are a source of some animosity between Athens and the rest of the country.

Why don't you slide that tzatziki this way.

*Ya FEH-reh toh **dza-dzee-KEE** ah-poh-thoh.*

Για φέρε το **τζατζίκι** από 'δώ.

The moussaka didn't turn out well.

*Then tohn PEH-tee-ha toh **moo-sa-KA**.*

Δεν τον πέτυχα το **μουσακά**.

This is probably the most classic of Hellenic home cooking. Basically a Greek lasagna, moussaka is one of the all-time classic dishes that you'll find on a Greek dinner table.

The kids want pastitsio.

*Ta peth-YA THEH-loo-nee **pas-TEE-tsyo**.*

Τα παιδιά θέλουνε **παστίτσιο**.

Just like μουσακά minus the eggplant.

My mom makes unbelievable gemista.

*EE MA-na moo KA-nee ah-PEES-tef-ta **yeh-mees-TA**.*

Η μάνα μου κάνει απίστευτα **γεμιστά**.

Γεμιστά are an assortment of vegetables, like tomatoes, zucchini, and bell peppers, stuffed with seasoned rice and baked in the oven. Drizzle olive oil over them, get a side of feta, and you will die from a foodgasm.

I ate all the dolmas.

*Eh-FA-gha OH-loos toos **dol-MA-thez**.*

Έφαγα όλους τους **ντολμάδες**.

Is there any bread left?

*Eh-hee MEE-nee ka-THOH-loo **psoh-MEE**?*

Έχει μείνει καθόλου **ψωμί**;

I just want half a **pita**.
*Mee-SEE **PEE-ta** THEH-loh MOH-noh.*
Μισή **πίτα** θέλω μόνο.

Should we order more french fries?
*Na pa-ra-GEE-loo-meh KYA-less **pa-TA-tess tee-gha-nee-TESS**?*
Να παραγγείλουμε κι άλλες **πατάτες τηγανιτές**;

I would kill for some spetsofai.
*Thah SKOH-toh-na yia LEE-yho **speh-dzoh-FA-ee**.*
Θα σκότωνα για λίγο **σπετζοφάι**.

The traditional dish from the town of Volos, *spetsofai* is hot peppers and spicy sausage in tomato sauce. Just add a rustic loaf of bread to the equation and you're good.

I burned the bean stew.
*EH-ka-psa tee **fa-soh-LA-tha**.*
Έκαψα τη **φασολάδα**.

Nice and heavy, this stuff's perfect on a cold day.

····Meat
KREH-ahs
Κρέας

Greeks love meat! Pork, beef, lamb, ribs, you name it. If you're hardcore enough, try the lamb innards, beef brain, or tongue.

Let's order some...
Na pa-ra-GEE-loo-meh...
Να παραγγείλουμε...

> **beef.**
> *mohs-HA-ree.*
> μοσχάρι.

> **pork.**
> *hee-ree-NOH.*
> χοιρινό.

YUM!))

mmmmmm!
MMMMMMMM!

Damn, this meatball is tasty!
Pssss FEE-leh, yef-stee-KO-ta-tohs oh kef-TESS!
Πσσσς φίλε, **γευστικότατος** ο κεφτές!

Your mom makes the best tzatziki ever.
EE MA-na soo KA-nee toh ka-LEE-the-roh tza-TZEE-kee.
Η μάνα σου κάνει **το καλύτερο** τζατζίκι.

My compliments to the chef.
Ta see-nhah-ree-TEE-riah-A-moo ston MA-yee-ra.
Τα συγχαρητήριά μου στον μάγειρα.

Delicious!
Peh-da-NOH-stee-mo!
Πεντανόστιμο!

Baller!
Tzee-TZEE!
Τζιτζί!

Bomb!
Tzet!
Τζετ!
Literally, "jet."

Scrumptious!
Noh-stee-MOH-ta-toh!
Νοστιμότατο!

Can I have seconds?
Boh-ROH nah EH-ho EH-na DEH-fte-roh GEE-roh?
Μπορώ να έχω ένα δεύτερο γύρο;

lamb.
ahr-NEE.
αρνί.

chicken.
ko-TOH-poo-loh.
κοτόπουλο.

ribs.
pa-ee-THA-kya.
παϊδάκια.

ground beef.
Beef-TEH-kya.
μπιφτέκια.

innards.
Koh-koh-REH-tsee.
κοκορέτσι.

More specifically, skewered innards wrapped with intestine.
Not for everyone.

····Seafood
Psah-ree-KA
Ψαρικά

Greeks generally like smaller fish because they have more
flavor. All varieties are either grilled or fried and eaten with lots
of lemon. Here are the most popular items on the menu, but
don't forget to ask what the catch of the day is.

Is this fish fresh?
*EE-neh FRESS-koh toh **PSA-ree**?*
Είναι φρέσκο το **ψάρι**;

Can I get grilled/fried...
Boh-ROH na EH-hoh psee-TOH/tee-gha-nee-TOH...
Μπορώ να έχω ψητό/τηγανητό...

smelt.

ma-ree-THA-kee.

μαριδάκι.

Deep-fried whole and served in a basket, these things are TINY. They're basically fish fries.

calamari.

ka-la-MA-ree.

καλαμάρι.

Fried calamari is usually referred to as καλαμαράκια (*ka-la-ma-RA-kya*).

octopus.

hta-POH-thee.

χταπόδι.

crab salad.

ka-voo-roh-sa-LA-ta.

καβουροσαλάτα.

shrimp.

yha-REE-thes.

γαρίδες.

lobster.

ah-sta-KOS.

αστακός.

mussels.
MEE-thya.
μύδια.

sardines.
sar-THEH-les.
σαρδέλες.
The actual fish, not the fillets from the tin cans.

red mullet.
bar-BOO-nya.
μπαρμπούνια.
This fish is really good pan-fried.

bream.
tsee-POO-ra.
τσιπούρα.
A white fish served grilled with lots of lemon.

Sea bass.
la-VRA-kee.
λαβράκι.
A white fish usually prepared either on the grill or in a soup.

What is the catch of the day?
Tee PSAH-ree-ah pee-AH-sah-the SEE-me-ra?
Τι ψάρια πιάσατε σήμερα;

····Restaurants
E-stee-ah-TOH-ree-ah
Εστιατόρια

Food is big business in Greece. You'll find everything from greasy 24-hour diners to five-star restaurants. Greeks eat late, so if someone invites you to dinner, be prepared to stay out till way past midnight. They mostly prefer traditional Greek restaurants called tavernas, but you can also find a great variety of haute and ethnic cuisine restaurants.

GROSS!)))
ЧІЯНКІ
ΓΙΑΚ!

This food is **nasty**!
*ΕΕ-neh **HAH-lya** toh fa-yee-TOH!*
Είναι **χάλια** το φαγητό!

I can't eat that.
Then boh-ROH na toh FA-oh af-TOH.
Δεν μπορώ να το φάω αυτό.

Dude, this is **disgusting**!
*Ma-LA-ka, **ahee-THEE-ah** EE-neh!*
Μαλάκα, **αηδία** είναι!

Don't eat that, it'll make you **puke**.
*Meen toh fas af-TOH, thah **kse-RA-sees**.*
Μη το φας αυτό, θα **ξεράσεις**.

Man, that gyro **did not sit well**.
*Poh, **then EH-ka-tse ka-LA** toh soo-VLAH-kee.*
Μην, **δεν έκατσε καλά** το σουβλάκι.

Dude, the Chinese food was good, but it gave me mad **indigestion**.
*Reh FEE-leh, ka-loh to Kee-NEH-zee-ko, ah-LA moo EH-feh-reh **ka-OO-ress**.*
Ρε φίλε, καλό το κινέζικο, αλλά μου έφερε **καούρες**.

Where do you want to eat?
Poo THEH-lees na FA-meh?
Πού θέλεις να φάμε;

Let's go to the...
PAH-me steen/stoh...
Πάμε στην/στο...

tavern.
ta-VER-na.
ταβέρνα.

The aforementioned traditional Greek restaurants. Get ready for the meat.

grill.
psee-stah-ree-AH.
ψησταριά.

fish tavern.
psa-roh-ta-VER-na.
ψαροταβέρνα.

There are a ton of fish taverns on all the islands, especially in Athens's main port, Piraeus.

gyro shack.
soo-vla-DZEE-thee-ko.
σουβλατζίδικο.

Greek people love gyro and souvlaki. You will find these places full, 24/7. They are the cheapest and most delicious fast-food restaurants, and you'll find one on almost every corner.

canteen. / roach coach.
kahn-DEE-na. / VROH-mee-ko.
καντίνα. / βρόμικο.

This is the Greek version of a food truck, offering hot dogs, french fries, and sometimes souvlaki kalamaki, and just like in the U.S., the shadier the neighborhood, the better the roach coach. In Athens, the best and most famous one is in Μαβίλη (*Ma-VEE-lee*) square, right next to the U.S. Embassy! After a crazy night out, at 5 o'clock in the morning the roach coaches are where it's at.

That **waitress** is such a bitch.
*Po-LEE poo-TA-nah ee **ser-vee-TOH-ra** mas.*
Πολύ πουτάνα η **σερβιτόρα** μας.

Our **waiter** was really quick.
*EE-tan poh-LEE GHREE-gho-rohs oh **ser-vee-TOH-rohs** mas.*
Ήταν πολύ γρήγορος ο **σερβιτόρος** μας.

The **service** is shit.
*Ya tohn POO-tsoh toh **SER-vees**.*
Για τον πούτσο το **σέρβις**.

Have you seen the **menu**?
*EH-heh-the thee tohn **ka-TA-loh-gho**?*
Έχετε δει τον **κατάλογο**;

What do you recommend?
TEE proh-TEE-ne-te?
Τι προτείνετε;

Did you leave a tip?
*AH-fee-sess **poor-boo-AHR**?*
Άφησες **πουρμπουάρ**;

People don't really tip much in Greece. Most just leave the change. But the funny thing is that the servers know Americans tip well, and they get really pissed if the tourists don't.

····Cheese
Tee-REE
Τυρί

Cheddar used to make everything better until I discovered feta. Crumble some on your fries — you'll flip your shit. Everybody knows feta, and it's definitely worth knowing, but there are a few other offerings that should not be overlooked.

Don't forget the feta.
*Meen xeh-HA-sees tee **FEH-ta**.*
Μην ξεχάσεις τη **φέτα**.

This kasseri is the business.
*SKEH-tee KA-vla toh **ka-SHE-ree**.*
Σκέτη καύλα το **κασέρι**.

Κασέρι is a sharp cheese that's great fried, grilled, or straight out the box.

I can't eat too much kefalotiri.
*Then boh-ROH na FA-oh poh-LEE **ke-fa-loh-TEE-ree**.*
Δεν μπορώ να φάω πολύ **κεφαλοτύρι**.

Super-salty but very flavorful. Good stuff.

I had really good mizithra in Crete.
*EH-fa-yha po-LEE ka-LEE **mee-ZEE-thra** steen KREE-tee.*
Έφαγα πολύ καλή **μυζήθρα** στην Κρήτη.

This is a very soft, spreadable, salty cheese. The unsalted version is ανθότυρο (*ahn-THOH-tee-roh*).

I'M FULL)))

HOHR-TA-SA
ΧΟΡΤΑΣΑ

I'm stuffed!
EH-ska-sa!
Έσκασα!

How could I eat so much!?
Pohs EH-fa-gha EH-tsee!?
Πώς έφαγα έτσι;

I can't eat anymore.
Then boh-ROH na FA-oh AH-loh.
Δεν μπορώ να φάω άλλο.

I can't take another **bite**.
*Then boh-ROH na FA-oh AH-lee **boo-KYA**.*
Δεν μπορώ να φάω άλλη **μπουκιά**.

Fuck, I'm going to **explode**.
*Ma-LA-ka, thah **SKA-soh**.*
Μαλάκα, θα **σκάσω**.

I'll yak if I even see food.
AH-ma thoh fa-yee-TOH, thah kse-RA-soh.
Άμα δω φαγητό, θα ξεράσω.

I've got a nice food baby going.
Thah yeh-NEE-soh.
Θα γεννήσω.
Literally, "I'm going to give birth."

I fucked this food up!
Gha-MEE-theeh-ka stoh fa-yee-TOH!
Γαμήθηκα στο φαγητό!

I ate all the **saganaki**.
*EH-fa-yha OH-loh toh **sa-gha-NA-kee**.*
Έφαγα όλο το **σαγανάκι**.
Fried cheese. 'Nuff said.

Where can I find a decent **halloumi**?

*Poo boh-ROH na vroh EH-na **ha-LOO-mee** tees proh-koh-PEES?*

Πού μπορώ να βρω ένα **χαλούμι** της προκοπής;

The national cheese of Cyprus, halloumi has a unique, salty taste and a spongy texture that's difficult to explain. You'll either love it or hate it, but its definitely work a try. This cheese is great grilled.

Do you know how to make **cheese salad**?

*KSEH-rees na FTYA-hnees **tee-roh-sa-LA-ta**?*

Ξέρεις να φτιάχνεις **τυροσαλάτα**;

More of a dip or spread than a salad, τυροσαλάτα goes great with bread, fries, and pita. The spicy version is called τυροκαυτερή (*tee-roh-kaf-teh-REE*).]

OLIVES)))
EH-LEE-ES
ΕΛΙΕΣ

Olive trees are everywhere in the country, so olives and olive oil are some of the main ingredients in Greek cuisine. Bread with olive oil and olives—it's so simple but so damn good.

Kalamon olives
Eh-lee-ES Kah-lah-MOHN
Ελιές Καλαμών
The most famous olives, huge and black, from the area of Kalamata, in Peloponnesus.

Green olives
PRAH-see-ness Eh-lee-ES
Πράσινες ελιές

••••Fruits
FROO-tah
Φρούτα

In the U.S., you know what fruit is supposed to taste like, but somehow the stuff from the store is just never right? That's because our shit is artificial, genetically modified garbage. In

Greece, it's all fresh and delicious and actually tastes the way nature said it should.

I want...
THEH-loh...
Θέλω...

apples.
MEE-la.
μήλα.

pears.
ahh-LA-thya.
αχλάδια.
The brown ones are the best.

oranges.
por-toh-KAL-ya.
πορτοκάλια.

grapes.
sta-FEE-lya.
σταφύλια.
Greek wine isn't known for being good, but the grapes sure are.

strawberries.
FRA-oo-les.
φράουλες.

figs.
SEE-ka.
σύκα.
Greek figs are ridiculously good. Don't forget to get your fix before you leave.

watermelon.
kar-POO-zee.
καρπούζι.
They eat a shit-ton of watermelon in Greece, especially in the summer.

cantaloupe.
peh-POH-nee.
πεπόνι.

Chop them all up and make a fruit salad.
KOHPS-ta OH-la ke KA-neh MEE-ah froo-toh-sa-LA-ta.
Κόψ' τα όλα και κάνε μία **φρουτοσαλάτα**.

····Vegetables
La-ha-nee-KA
Λαχανικά

You can't forget the veggies. Something's got to balance out all that meat and cheese. Here are the basics.

Don't forget to add…
Meen xeh-HA-sees na VA-lees…
Μην ξεχάσεις να βάλεις...

tomatoes.
doh-MA-tes.
ντομάτες.

onion.
kreh-MEE-thee.
κρεμμύδι.

string beans.
fa-soh-LA-kya.
φασολάκια.

corn.
ka-la-BOH-kee.
καλαμπόκι.

carrots.
ka-ROH-ta.
καρότα.

peas.
bee-ZEL-ya.
μπιζέλια.

Pies)))

ΠΙΤΕΣ

Don't think of your grandma's apple pie, now, that's not what
we're talking about. Greek pies are made with flaky, phyllo
dough and filled with a wide variety of sweet and savory
ingredients.

I want a piece of . . .
THEH-loh EH-na koh-MA-teeE
Θέλω ένα κομμάτι...

cheese pie.
tee-ROH-pee-ta.
τυρόπιτα.

kasseri pie.
kah-seh-ROH-pee-ta.
κασερόπιτα.
Kasseri is a super salty
cheese.

spinach pie.
spa-na-KOH-pee-ta.
σπανακόπιτα.

leek pie.
pra-SOH-pee-ta.
πρασόπιτα.

sausage roll.
loo-ka-nee-KOH-pee-ta.
λουκανικόπιτα.

ham and cheese pie.
*za-boh-noh-tee-ROH-
pee-ta.*
ζαμπονοτυρόπιτα.

potato pie.
pa-ta-TOH-pee-ta.
πατατόπιτα.

meat pie.
kreh-ah-TOH-pee-ta.
κρεατόπιτα.

apple pie.
mee-LOH-pee-tah.
μηλόπιτα.

milk pie.
yha-la-kto-BOO-reh-koh.
γαλακτομπούρεκο.
This is a phyllo-based
dessert filled with cream
and drenched in syrup.

custard pie.
boo-YHA-tsa.
μπουγάτσα.
μπουγάτσα is a phyllo-
based pie filled with custard
cream. Great in the morning
with a cup of coffee, or at
night with whatever else
you want to chase it with.

You didn't eat any...
Then EH-fa-yes ka-THOH-loo...
Δεν έφαγες καθόλου...

> **salad.**
> *sal-AH-ta.*
> σαλάτα.

> **tomato salad.**
> *doh-ma-toh-sa-LA-ta.*
>
> ντοματοσαλάτα.
>
> The best salad in the word, the Greek tomato salad is more commonly called χωριάτικη (*hor-YA-tee-kee*), which translates to village, or rustic salad. The authentic version contains no lettuce, unlike at most Greek restaurants in the U.S.

> **dako salad.**
> *DA-kos.*
>
> ντάκος.
>
> This is the traditional salad of the island of Crete. It's very similar to tomato salad but includes croutons and mizithra cheese instead of feta.

> **eggplant salad.**
> *meh-lee-dza-noh-sa-LA-ta.*
>
> μελιτζανοσαλάτα.
>
> Like the cheese salad mentioned earlier, this is more of a dip than an actual salad. It goes great with pita and fries.

> **potato salad.**
> *pa-ta-toh-sa-LA-ta.*
>
> πατατοσαλάτα.

••••Fast Food
FAHST-food
Φαστ Φουντ

When I mention fast food in Greece, I'm not just talking about burgers and fries. The streets of Athens are hiding a myriad of quick culinary selections. You'll find everything from the classic Mickey D's all the way to some questionable places that serve nothing more than meat on a stick. And the best part is most of them are open super late.

Here, take half of my **sandwich**.
*EH-la PA-reh mee-SOH ap-toh **SAHD-weets** moo.*
Έλα πάρε μισό απ' το **σάντουίτς** μου.

Can you make me a **grilled cheese**?
*Boh-REES na moo KA-nees EH-na **tohst**?*
Μπορείς να μου κάνεις ένα **τοστ**;

Grilled cheese sandwiches have been a popular quick and easy meal option in Greece for years. Usually made with Gouda, you can get them with or without ham from any café in the country.

We're all going for **crêpes**.
*PA-meh OH-lee yia **KREH-pes**.*
Πάμε όλοι για **κρέπες**.

I know they're French, but crêpes are a fucking art form in Greece. This is by far my favorite late-night munchy. You can go sweet or savory, and you get to watch them make it right in front of your drunk ass. It's like Subway but you actually eat fresh!

Are we going to **McDonald's** or **Goody's**?
*PA-meh **mahk-DOH-nalts** ee **GOO-deez**?*
Πάμε **Μακντόναλτς** ή **Γκούντιζ**;

Goody's is a Greek fast-food burger chain and it's way more popular than McDonald's. It's not health food by any means, but it's definitely better quality than American fast food choices. McDonald's is also called Μακ (Mahk) for short.

Let's go get something from the **roach coach**.
*PA-meh na FA-meh EH-na **VROH-mee-koh**.*
Πάμε να φάμε ένα **βρόμικο**.

Do we have time to go to Everest real quick?
*Proh-la-VEH-noo-meh na PA-meh EH-vehr-est sta
YHREE-yho-ra?*
Προλαβαίνουμε να πάμε Έβερεστ στα γρήγορα;
Everest is a 24-hour sandwich-and-coffee chain. It also has a
huge selection of phyllo pies. This is the best place to go when
you only have a few minutes to grab a bite.

····Sweets
Ylee-KAH
Γλυκά

Everybody likes the sweet stuff. Here are some of the most
popular and traditional desserts for you to overindulge in when
you're in Greece.

**Get me some chocolate 'cuz I haven't fucked in
months.**
*FEH-reh moo LEE-yee soh-koh-LA-ta ya-TEE EH-hoh
ah-yha-MEE-es.*
Φέρε μου λίγη σοκολάτα γιατί έχω αγαμίες.

My stomach hurts from all that candy.
*Meh poh-NA-ee toh stoh-MA-hee moo ap-OH-less tees
ka-ra-MEH-les.*
Με πονάει το στομάχι μου απ' όλες τις καραμέλες.

Were you the one that ate all the cookies?
Eh-SEE EH-fa-yes OH-la ta bee-SKOH-ta?
Εσύ έφαγες όλα τα μπισκότα;

I want more ice cream.
THEH-loh KYA-loh pa-yhoh-TOH.
Θέλω κι άλλο παγωτό.

C'mon, hurry up and get me a piece of baklava!
*AH-deh, teh-LEE-oh-ne ke FEH-reh moo EH-na koh-MA-
tee ba-kla-VA!*
Άντε, τελείωνε και φέρε μου ένα κομμάτι μπακλαβά!
Baklava just might be the best thing in the world.

Wait, the rice pudding is still hot.
*Peh-REE-meh-neh, KEH-ee ah-KOH-ma toh **ree-ZOH-yha-loh**.*
Περίμενε, καίει ακόμα το **ρυζόγαλο**.

Can I have a spoon of preserves with my coffee?
*Boh-ROH na EH-hoh EH-na **ylee-KOH too koo-tal-yoo** meh tohn ka-FEH moo?*
Μπορώ να έχω ένα **γλυκό του κουταλιού** με τον καφέ μου;

Preserves are essentially very sweet fruit jams. The fruit is more whole than in jam and served on a small plate with a teaspoon. This is a very traditional, rustic, old-fashioned dessert.

I haven't had a submarine in years.
*Eh-HOH HROH-nya na FA-oh **ee-poh-VREE-hee-oh**.*
Έχω χρόνια να φάω **υποβρύχιο**.

Another traditional sweet, a submarine is a vanilla-flavored paste that's scooped onto a spoon and served in a glass of water to soften it up. It sounds really weird, but it's actually very good.

I don't really like halva.
*Then moo poh-lee-ah-REH-see oh **hahl-VAS**.*
Δεν μου πολυαρέσει ο **χαλβάς**.

Halva is a nut butter and tahini based confection that can be found in various forms throughout Eastern Europe and the Middle East. It's also loaded with sugar and usually served with Greek coffee.

Get me another piece of ravani.
*FEH-reh moo KYAH-loh EH-na koh-MA-tee **ra-va-NEE**.*
Φέρε μου κι άλλο κομμάτι **ραβανί**.

Ravani is a classic Greek coffee cake that's absolutely soaked in syrup. Delicious.

My ex used to go crazy for tiramisu.
*EE PROH-een moo treh-leh-NOH-tan ya **tee-ra-mee-SOO**.*
Η πρώην μου τρελαινόταν για **τιραμισού**.

····Acknowledgments

I would like to thank my parents. The most rewarding part of this experience has been the all-too-rare chance to make you proud. I am eternally grateful.

Thanks Sonia. You're my favorite.

····About the Author

Christos Samaras spent his early years in Oakland, California, but made an impromptu decision to run off to his family's native Greece for a change of scenery and a much-needed shock to his sheltered system. Brilliantly disguising and legitimizing an escape plan in a bid for higher education abroad, he was able to disappear for a Red Bull– and Marlboro Lights–fueled romp in Europe's southeastern peninsula. Aimlessly meandering through a marketing communications degree allows for plenty of free time to distract oneself with more eccentric pursuits which offer, among other things, the uncanny opportunity to practice the art of speaking like the best of the worst Greek sailors. After all, the greatest stories are usually told with the dirtiest vocabulary. His most engaging interests, which helped keep him away from the classroom, still include the tireless pursuit of driving perfection, good conversation at impossible hours, Greek soccer, no matter how bad it is, and chasing an insane dream of one last grand adventure in the darkest, dingiest, most wonderful part of Old Europe. Christos is back in his hometown of Oakland but he is still on the hunt for a place that sports politics as groovy as Sweden and a view as badass as Greece.